Cycling in the
North of
England

Rupert Douglas
with John Grimshaw CBE

Editor: Donna Wood
Designer: Phil Barfoot
Copy Editor: Helen Ridge
Proofreader: Judith Forshaw
Picture Researchers: Alice Earle (AA)
and Jonathan Bewley (Sustrans)
Image retouching and internal repro:
Sarah Montgomery and James Tims
Cartography provided by the Mapping Services
Department of AA Publishing from data supplied by
Richard Sanders and Sustrans mapping team
Research and development by: Lindsey Ryle, Melissa
Henry, Julian Hunt and Sustrans' regional staff
Supplementary text: Nick Cotton, James Adamson
and Josh Learner
Production: Lorraine Taylor

Produced by AA Publishing

ISBN: 978-0-7495-7250-1

Published by AA Publishing (a trading name of
AA Media Limited, whose registered office is
Fanum House, Basing View, Basingstoke
RG21 4EA; registered number 06112600).

A04632

Free cycling permits are required on some British
Waterways canal towpaths. Visit www.waterscape.com
or call 0845 671 5530.

The National Cycle Network has been made possible
by the support and co-operation of hundreds of
organisations and thousands of individuals, including:
local authorities and councils, central governments
and their agencies, the National Lottery, landowners,
utility and statutory bodies, countryside and
regeneration bodies, the Landfill Communities Fund,
other voluntary organisations, charitable trusts and
foundations, the cycle trade and industry, corporate
sponsors, community organisations and Sustrans'
supporters. Sustrans would also like to extend thanks
to the thousands of volunteers who generously
contribute their time to looking after their local
sections of the Network.

Printed and bound in Dubai by Oriental Press
theAA.com/shop

Sustrans
2 Cathedral Square
College Green
Bristol BS1 5DD
www.sustrans.org.uk

Sustrans is a Registered Charity in the UK:
Number 326550 (England and Wales)
SCO39263 (Scotland).

CONTENTS

THE RIDES

It was on my bike,
I came up with des

Foreword by **Wayne Hemingway MBE,** designer

I recently set off on one of my cycling expeditions which involved getting to the start point by train. I asked at the ticket office if pushbikes were allowed on all trains at that particular time of day. The young man behind the counter looked at me blankly and said "What's a pushbike?" Granted, adding the word 'push' before bike may be a little old school but it did seem to sum up how Britain has been through a strange period when it comes to cycling. A period where many forgot how wonderful it is to get on your pushbike, when many became wedded to the car, where for the vast majority a 'ride in the countryside' meant getting in the family saloon, turning the air conditioning on and hermetically sealing yourself from the world.

"A 'ride in the countryside' meant getting in the family saloon, turning the air conditioning on and hermetically sealing yourself from the world"

Those of us that do get on our bikes do understand the many levels of joy, discovery, good health, thrift and, nowadays, the self-congratulation we can give ourselves for doing our environmental bit. Increasingly, often due to the good work of Sustrans, we can cycle safely, well away from the 'lumps in lumps of metal' and this book helps you navigate a number of wonderful routes.

I was born in Morecambe and have family around there. I know that I am 'home' when in spring I cycle the Crook o'Lune into Lancaster and get high on the pungent wild garlic that carpets the woods along the route, stopping off at the picturesque Penny Bridge to watch the kingfishers and then popping into my Auntie Jacquie and Uncle David's house in the lovely little village of Halton. It was on my bike, as it often is, that I came up with design ideas and as an urban designer spot 'opportunities' like the amazing old mills in Luneside, Lancaster that deserve bringing back to life.

On a recent visit to Blackpool, to talk at a regeneration conference, I hired a bike and did the Blackpool North Shore to Fleetwood route. Getting 'down and dirty' with the problems that Blackpool has really crystallized my thoughts and importantly allowed me to enjoy all four courses of the conference dinner.

Looking at the routes in this book, I want to do them all. My recent Coast to Coast ride has left me wanting to do more routes in and around Whitehaven and the Lakes, and to explore Northumberland and the North East coast. The exciting new architecture and renewed Scouse swagger deserves a closer look from the Liverpool Loopline, and if I do that then I might as well do the Fallowfield Loop... I will do these and more... if I don't get them done soon I retire in 20 years or so... so plenty of time then...

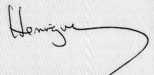

"Looking at the routes in this book, I want to do them all"

INTRODUCTION

Much of the countryside of the North of England is in either a National Park or an Area of Outstanding Natural Beauty (AONB). Pretty rugged and remote some of it is, too, and not the natural terrain for family-friendly bike rides. But around the fringes of its mountains and moorland, along stretches of its stunning coastline, its cleverly graded canal towpaths and reclaimed railway lines, there are plenty of pedal-powered adventures that thankfully don't require a Tour de France (or of Britain) level of fitness.

Blackpool Tower and Pleasure Beach

Both Irish Sea and North Sea coasts feature strongly in many of the rides in this guide. On those from Berwick-upon-Tweed and Alnmouth in the Northumberland Coast AONB, you'll get a taste of the Coast & Castles Cycle Route, which runs for nearly 400 miles (644km) between Newcastle, Edinburgh and Aberdeen.

Further south, lovely stretches of the Cleveland and the North Yorkshire Moors National Park coastlines can be explored between the seaside resorts of Redcar and Saltburn, and Scarborough and Whitby. There's also a ride between lighthouses along National Trust-owned coastline and across the Tyne estuary.

Across on the Irish Sea coast, sandy Sefton Coast at Southport is reached on a ride from Liverpool's famous Aintree racecourse, and you can follow the Fylde Coast from Blackpool's North Pier to Fleetwood on a traffic-free beachside route.

Much quieter, and with great views across to the Scottish coastline of Dumfries & Galloway, is the ride on the Solway Coast AONB, west of Carlisle. This is also part of Hadrian's Wall World Heritage Site and Hadrian's Cycleway, another section of which gives you a ride along the River Tyne nearer to Newcastle.

There's a ride inland from the coastal town of Morecambe up the Lune Valley, part of a new Way of the Roses coast-to-coast cycle route across Lancashire and Yorkshire. Then there are rides inland, from coastal Whitehaven and Sunderland, which are at either end of the Sea-to-Sea (C2C), Britain's most popular long-distance cycle route.

Lake Windermere
and Ambleside

Millennium and Tyne
Bridges, Newcastle

Robin Hood's Bay

Cycling to the coast is part of the appeal of rides from the Lake District gateway town of Kendal along a section of the Walney to Wear & Whitby (W2W) cycle route, and from the maritime city of Hull on a section of the Trans Pennine Trail, which is a largely traffic-free coast-to-coast route between Hornsea and Southport. Some of its riverside sections further inland can be explored on several rides in this guide.

Traversing the 'spine of England' in a different way is the Pennine Cycleway, running for over 350 miles (563km) between Derby and Berwick-upon-Tweed. A relatively easy section of it can be pedalled using the towpath of the Leeds & Liverpool Canal in Pendle country to the edge of the Yorkshire Dales National Park. This same canal gives an excellent ride out of Leeds through the Aire Valley. Greenway rides from, to and around other historic and culturally rich cities, such as Chester, York, Huddersfield, Manchester, Middlesbrough and Liverpool, complete the picture of the fascinating heritage as well as the scenic splendour of the North of England. The National Cycle Network plays a vital role in linking them for cycle and walk.

Finally, keep an eye out for some of the magnificent artwork and sculptures on the Network, including David Kemp's *King Cole* near Sunderland, Peter Rogers' *Fisher of Dreams* on the Naburn swing bridge near York, and Alan Dawson's *Phoenix Bridge* at Cleator Moor, near Whitehaven. And don't forget to stop for well-earned refreshments, locally baked, brewed or otherwise, en route.

NATIONAL CYCLE NETWORK FACTS & FIGURES

Most of the routes featured here are part of the National Cycle Network. The aim of this book is to enable you to sample some of the highlights of the region on two wheels, but the rides given here are really just a taster, as there are more than 13,000 miles of Network throughout the UK to explore. More than three-quarters of us live within two miles of one of the routes.

Over one million journeys a day are made on the National Cycle Network; for special trips like fun days out and holiday bike rides, but also the necessary everyday trips; taking people to school, to work, to the shops, to visit each other and to seek out green spaces. Half of these journeys are made on foot and half by bike, with urban traffic-free sections of the Network seeing the most usage.

The National Cycle Network is host to one of the UK's biggest collections of public art. Sculptures, benches, water fountains, viewing points and award-winning bridges enhance its pathways, making Sustrans one of the most prolific commissioners of public art in the UK.

The Network came into being following the award of the first-ever grant from the lottery, through the Millennium Commission, in 1995. Funding for the Network also came from bike retailers and manufacturers through the Bike Hub, as well as local authorities and councils UK-wide, and Sustrans' many supporters. Over 2,500 volunteer Rangers give their time to Sustrans to assist in the maintenance of the National Cycle Network by adopting sections of route in communities throughout the UK. They remove glass and litter, cut back vegetation and try to ensure routes are well signed.

Developing and maintaining the National Cycle Network is just one of the ways in which Sustrans pursues its vision of a world in which people can choose to travel in ways that benefit their health and the environment.

We hope that you enjoy using this book to explore the paths and cycleways of the National Cycle Network and we would like to thank the many hundreds of organisations who have worked with Sustrans to develop the walking and cycling routes, including every local authority and council in the UK.

MAP LEGEND

Traffic Free/On Road route · Ride Start or Finish Point · National Cycle Network (Traffic Free) · National Cycle Network (On Road)

PH	AA recommended pub
	Abbey, cathedral or priory
	Abbey, cathedral or priory in ruins
	Aquarium
	Aqueduct or viaduct
	Arboretum
	Battle site
	Bird Reserve (RSPB)
	Cadw (Welsh Heritage) site
	Campsite
	Caravan site
	Caravan & campsite
	Castle
	Cave
	Country park
	English Heritage site
	Farm or animal centre
	Garden
	Hill-fort
	Historic house
	Industrial attraction
	Marina
	Monument
	Museum or gallery
	National Nature Reserve: England, Scotland, Wales
	Local nature reserve
	National Trust property
	National Trust for Scotland property
	Picnic site
	Roman remains
	Steam railway
	Theme park
	Tourist Information Centre
	Viewpoint
	Visitor or heritage centre
	World Heritage Site (UNESCO)
	Zoo or wildlife collection
	AA golf course
	Stadium
	Indoor Arena
	Tennis
	Horse racing
	Rugby Union
	Football
	Athletics
	Motorsports
	County cricket

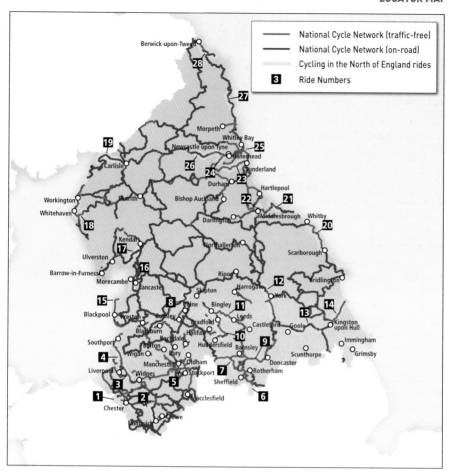

National Cycle Network (traffic-free)
National Cycle Network (on-road)
Cycling in the North of England rides
3 Ride Numbers

KEY TO LOCATOR MAP

1	Chester to Hawarden Bridge	15	Fylde Coast: Blackpool to Fleetwood
2	South Cheshire: Nantwich to Chester	16	Lune Valley
3	Liverpool Loopline: Halewood to Aintree	17	Kendal to Grange-over-Sands
4	Sefton Coast: Aintree to Southport	18	Rowrah to Whitehaven & Workington
5	Fallowfield Loop: South Manchester	19	Solway Coast from Burgh by Sands
6	Rother Valley Ride	20	Scarborough to Whitby
7	Upper Don Valley	21	Redcar to Saltburn-by-Sea
8	Pendle Country: Foulridge to Gargrave	22	Tees Bridges: From the Tees Barrage
9	Old Moor Nature Reserve to Sprotbrough	23	Roker Beach to Beamish Museum
10	Birkby Bradley, Calder Valley & Spen Valley Greenways	24	Derwent Walk & Gibside from Swalwell
11	Aire Valley Towpath: Leeds to Bingley	25	Souter to St Mary's
12	York to Selby & Beningbrough Hall	26	Tyne Riverside: Newburn to Corbridge
13	River Humber: Hessle to Howden	27	Alnmouth to Druridge Bay
14	Hornsea Rail Trail: Hull to Hornsea	28	Holy Island

CYCLING WITH CHILDREN

Kids love bikes and love to ride. Cycling helps them to grow up fit, healthy and independent, and introduces them to the wider world and the adventure it holds.

TOP TIPS FOR FAMILY BIKE RIDES:

- Take along snacks, drinks and treats to keep their energy and spirit levels up.
- Don't be too ambitious. It's much better that everyone wants to go out again, than all coming home exhausted, tearful and permanently put off cycling.
- Plan your trip around interesting stops and sights along the way. Don't make journey times any longer than children are happy to sit and play at home.
- Even on a fine day, take extra clothes and waterproofs – just in case. Check that trousers and laces can't get caught in the chain when pedalling along.
- Wrap up toddlers. When a young child is on the back of a bike, they won't be generating heat like the person doing all the pedalling!
- Be careful not to pinch their skin when putting their helmet on. It's easily done and often ends in tears. Just place your forefinger between the clip and the chin.
- Ride in a line with the children in the middle of the adults. If there's only one of you, the adult should be at the rear, keeping an eye on all the children in front. Take special care at road junctions.
- Check that children's bikes are ready to ride. Do the brakes and gears work? Is the saddle the right height? Are the tyres pumped up?
- Carry some sticking plasters and antiseptic wipes – kids are far more likely to fall off and graze arms, hands or knees.
- Take a camera to record the trip – memories are made of this.

TRANSPORTING YOUNG CHILDREN ON TWO WHEELS

It's now easier than ever for you to ride your bike with young children.

- Child seats: *6 months to five years (one child)*. Once a baby can support its own head (usually at 6–12 months) they can be carried in a child seat. Seats are fitted mainly to the rear of the bike.
- Trailers: babies to five years *(up to two children)*. Young babies can be strapped into their car seat and carried in a trailer, and older children can be strapped in and protected from the wind and rain.
- Tag-along trailer bikes: *approx four to nine years*. Tag-alongs (the back half of a child's bike attached to the back of an adult one) allow a child to be towed while they either add some of their own pedal power or just freewheel and enjoy the ride.
- Tow bar: *approx four to eight years*. A tow bar converts a standard child's bike to a trailer bike by lifting their front wheel from the ground to prevent them from steering, while enabling them to pedal independently. When you reach a safe place, the tow bar can be detached and the child's bike freed.

TEACHING YOUR CHILD TO RIDE

There are lots of ways for children to develop and gain cycling confidence before they head out on their own.

- Tricycles or trikes: available for children from ten months to five years old. They have pedals so kids have all the fun of getting around under their own steam.
- Balance bikes: are like normal bikes but without the pedals. This means children learn to balance, steer and gain confidence on two wheels while being able to place their feet firmly and safely on the ground.

- **Training wheels:** stabilisers give support to the rear of the bike and are the easiest way to learn to ride but potentially the slowest.

BUYING THE RIGHT BIKE FOR YOUR CHILD

Every child develops differently and they may be ready to learn to ride between the ages of three and seven. When children do progress to their own bike, emphasising the fun aspect will help them take the tumbles in their stride. Encouragement and praise are important to help them persevere.

Children's bikes generally fall into age categories based on the average size of a child of a specific age. There are no hard and fast rules, as long as your child isn't stretched and can reach the brakes safely and change gear easily. It's important to buy your child a bike that fits them rather than one they can grow into. Ask your local bike shop for advice and take your child along to try out different makes and sizes.

To find a specialist cycle retailer near you visit www.thecyclingexperts.co.uk

HOT TIPS & COOL TRICKS...

WHAT TO WEAR

For most of the rides featured in this book you do not need any special clothing or footwear. Shoes that are suitable for walking are also fine for cycling. Looser-fitting trousers allow your legs to move more freely, while tops with zips let you regulate your temperature. In cold weather, take gloves and a warm hat; it's also a good idea to pack a waterproof. If you are likely to be out at dusk, take a bright reflective top. If you start to cycle regularly, you may want to invest in some specialist equipment for longer rides, especially padded shorts and gloves.

WHAT TO TAKE

For a short ride, the minimum you will need is a pump and a small tool bag with a puncture repair kit, just in case. However, it is worth considering the following: water bottle, spare inner tube, 'multi-tool' (available from cycle shops), lock, money, sunglasses, lightweight waterproof (some pack down as small as a tennis ball), energy bars, map, camera and a spare top in case it cools down or to keep you warm when you stop for refreshments.

HOW TO TAKE IT

Rucksacks are fine for light loads but can make your back hot and sweaty. For heavier loads and for longer or more regular journeys, you are better off with panniers that attach to a bike rack.

BIKE ACCESSORIES

You may also want to invest in a helmet. A helmet will not prevent accidents from happening but can provide protection if you do fall off your bike. They are particularly recommended for young children. Ultimately, wearing a helmet is a question of individual choice and parents need to make that choice for their children.

A bell is a must for considerate cyclists. A friendly tinkle warns that you are approaching, but never assume others can hear you.

LOCKING YOUR BIKE

Unless you are sitting right next to your bike when you stop for refreshments, it is worth locking it, preferably to something immovable like a post, fence or railings (or a bike stand, of course). If nothing else, lock it to a companion's bike. Bike theft is more common in towns and cities, and if you regularly leave your bike on the streets, it is important to invest in a good-quality lock and to lock and leave your bike in a busy, well-lit location.

GETTING TO THE START OF A RIDE

The best rides are often those that you can do right from your doorstep, maximizing time on your bike and reducing travelling time. If you need to travel to the start of the ride, have you thought about catching a train?

FINDING OUT MORE – WWW.SUSTRANS.ORG.UK

Use the Sustrans website to find out where you can cycle to from home or while you are away on holiday, and browse through a whole host of other useful information.
Visit www.sustrans.org.uk

MAKING THE MOST OF YOUR BIKE

Making a few simple adjustments to your bike will make your ride more enjoyable and comfortable:

- **Saddle height:** raise or lower it so that you have good contact with your pedals (to make the most of your leg power) and so that you can always put a reassuring foot on the ground.
- **Saddle position:** getting the saddle in the right place will help you get the most from your pedal power without straining your body.
- **Handlebars:** well-positioned handlebars are crucial for your comfort and important for control of your steering and brakes.

...BIKE MAINTENANCE

Like any machine, a bike will work better and last longer if you care for it properly. Get in the habit of checking your bike regularly – simple checks and maintenance can help you have hassle-free riding and avoid repairs.

- **Tools:** there are specialist tools for specific tasks, but all you need to get started are: a pump, an old toothbrush, lubricants and grease, cleaning rags, a puncture repair kit, tyre levers, allen keys, screwdrivers and spanners.

REGULAR CHECKS

- **Every week:** Check tyres, brakes, lights, handlebars and seat are in good order and tightly secured.
- **Every month:** Wipe clean and lubricate chain with chain oil.
  Wipe the dirt from wheels.
  Check tread on tyres.
  Check brake pads.
  Check gear and brake cables and make sure that gears are changing smoothly.
- **Every year:** Take your bike to an experienced mechanic for a thorough service.
- **Tip:** If in doubt, leave it to the professionals. Bike mechanics are much more affordable than car mechanics, and some will even collect the bike from your home and return it to you when all the work is done.

FIXING A PUNCTURE

Punctures don't happen often and are easy to fix yourself. If you don't fancy repairing a puncture on your journey, carry a spare inner tube and a pump so you can change the tube, then fix the puncture when you get home.
If you don't mind repairing punctures when they happen, make sure you carry your repair kit and pump with you at all times. All puncture repair kits have full instructions with easy-to-follow pictures.

Alternatively, if you don't want to get your hands dirty, just visit your local bike shop and they will fix the puncture for you.

Regular checks and inspections

Mending a puncture: easy peasy

Yearly professional checks and servicing

CHESTER TO HAWARDEN BRIDGE

Chester is ringed by medieval walls, with fragments dating back to Saxon and even Roman times – on the south side of the city centre is the site of the Roman amphitheatre. The medieval town flourished as a port until the silting of the River Dee in the 15th century. It is the only city in England to have preserved its walls in their entirety, and they offer a 2-mile (3km) perimeter walk, with fine views of the city and the surrounding countryside.

Cycling is permitted along the towpath of the Shropshire Union Canal, which links the city centre to the railway path, an attractive open ride out into the surrounding farmland, planted with potatoes, maize and grain. The Mickle Trafford to Dee Marsh railway line once carried steel to and from the steelworks on the banks of the Dee at Hawarden Bridge. The ride crosses the tidal River Dee via the bridge and ends on the south bank of the river at Connah's Quay. At Hawarden Bridge, you may wish to try the alternative return route to Chester by following the excellent trail on the north bank of the River Dee (Regional Route 89) back into the city centre.

ROUTE INFORMATION

National Route: 5
Start: Shropshire Union Canal basin, off South View Road, or Chester train station.
Finish: Hawarden Bridge.

Distance: 6 miles (9.5km). Alternative option via River Dee 7 miles (11km).
Grade: Easy.
Surface: Tarmac.
Hills: None.

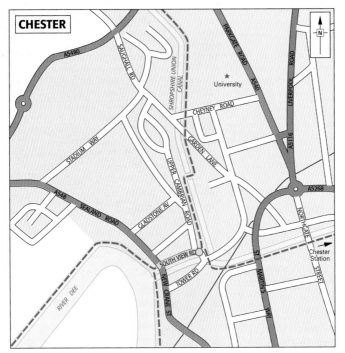

YOUNG & INEXPERIENCED CYCLISTS

Traffic-free, although you will need to use roads if you go for refreshments in Connah's Quay, beyond Hawarden Bridge.

REFRESHMENTS

• Lots of choice just off the route on the waymarked link to Chester city centre, including Telford's Warehouse pub at the end of the canal towpath.

The Old City Walls at Chester

THINGS TO SEE & DO

- **Chester Cathedral:** dating back to AD 660; 01244 324756; www.chestercathedral.com
- **Grosvenor Museum, Chester:** Roman archaeological finds, as well as displays on local history; 01244 402033; www.grosvenormuseum.co.uk
- **Chester Castle:** Agricola Tower and castle walls; www.english-heritage.org.uk
- **Chester Roman Amphitheatre:** www.english-heritage.org.uk

TRAIN STATIONS

Chester; Hawarden Bridge; Shotton.

BIKE HIRE

Enquire locally.

FURTHER INFORMATION

- To view or print National Cycle Network routes, visit www.sustrans.org.uk
- Maps for this area are available to buy from www.sustransshop.co.uk
- **Chester Tourist Information:** 01244 351609; www.visitchester.com

ROUTE DESCRIPTION

Starting at the Shropshire Union Canal basin off South View Road, follow the canal towpath

A peaceful cycleway near Chester

northwards towards the converted railway path. If you are starting from Chester train station, you can reach the path by crossing Station Road, turning right into Crewe Street, then left into Egerton Street and then right onto the canal towpath.

The railway path and the canal towpath meet near the water meadow at Abbot's Meads, and

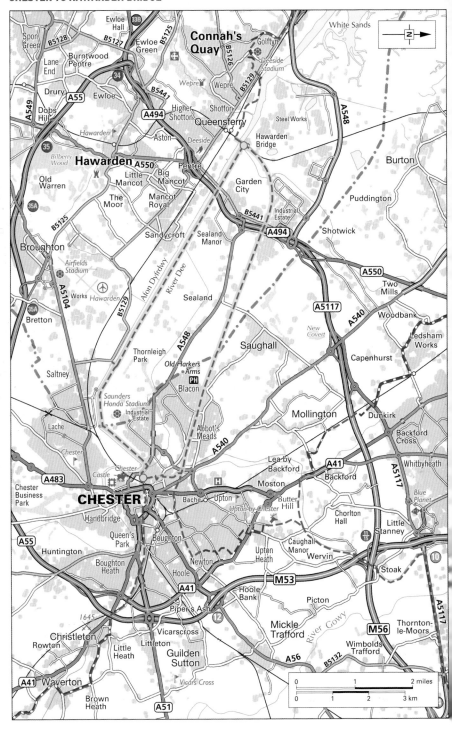

Cyclists crossing Hawarden Bridge

the ride continues along the railway path (National Route 5) through Blacon, crossing over the English/Welsh border and progressing out into farmland, with the Clwyd Hills making a picturesque backdrop.

The route for cyclists (and walkers) crosses the Dee at Hawarden Bridge on a new cantilevered structure funded by the local authorities. At the railway triangle at Dee Marsh, the northern leg leads to the Deeside employment zone. From here, you could get the train back from Shotton, or for a return journey, retrace the route back to Hawarden Bridge and take the riverside route alongside the River Dee back into Chester.

NEARBY CYCLE ROUTES

National Route 5 continues from Connah's Quay to the eastern outskirts of Flint, then resumes on-road to Prestatyn, where it continues traffic-free to the outskirts of Llandudno. The railway path is being extended eastwards from Hoole to Mickle Trafford.

Other waymarked or traffic-free rides include:
- Woodland paths in Delamere Forest Park, to the east of Chester.
- The Whitegate Way, a railway path just a little further east from Delamere.
- The Shropshire Union Canal between Chester and Ellesmere boat museum.

SOUTH CHESHIRE – NANTWICH TO CHESTER

This ride links together the two most historic settlements in Cheshire: Nantwich and Chester. Nantwich was established by the Romans who produced salt from the naturally occurring brine springs along the banks of the River Weaver. Over time, the town experienced a number of disasters, including being destroyed by Henry III, who wished to deny the Welsh the use of its salt, and the Great Fire of 1583, which destroyed almost all the town. But it was rebuilt again and today it's a fascinating place to visit and an attractive start for this ride.

Chester is one of Britain's great heritage cities. It was a Roman legionary headquarters, has almost complete city walls, a cathedral with some of the finest medieval carvings in Europe, a refectory with a magnificent modern glass west window, 700-year-old rows of shopping galleries and much more.

Most of the route follows relatively quiet roads through the rich farmlands of the Cheshire Plain until you pick up the towpath of the Shropshire Union Canal from Waverton into Chester. This is an easy place to end your ride, with numerous places to relax, including riverside cafes.

ROUTE INFORMATION

National Route: 45
Regional Route: 75
Start: Nantwich town centre.
Finish: Chester city centre or train station.
Distance: 24 miles (38.5km).
Grade: Easy.

Surface: Tarmac.
Hills: Some gentle hills.

YOUNG & INEXPERIENCED CYCLISTS

Nantwich riverside path and the canal towpath from Waverton to Chester are traffic-free, but the country lanes have some traffic and are suitable only for more confident cyclists.

REFRESHMENTS

• Lots of choice in Nantwich and Chester.

Sweet Briar Hall, Nantwich

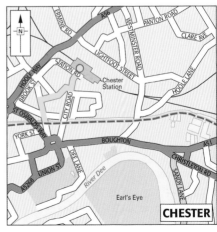

St Mary's Church, Nantwich

- Venetian Marina Cafe on the Shropshire Union Canal south of Cholmondeston.
- Boot & Slipper Inn, Wettenhall.
- Cafes in Tarporley.

THINGS TO SEE & DO
Nantwich:
- **Nantwich Museum:** exhibitions on the history of the ancient market town; 01270 627104; www.nantwichmuseum.org.uk

Chester:
- **Chester Cathedral:** beautiful building dating back to AD 660; 01244 324756; www.chestercathedral.com
- **Chester Zoo:** over 7,000 animals and 400 different species; 01244 380280; www.chesterzoo.org
- **Chester Roman Amphitheatre:** the largest uncovered amphitheatre in the UK; 01244 402260; www.english-heritage.org.uk

TRAIN STATIONS
Nantwich; Chester.

BIKE HIRE
- **South Cheshire Cycle Hire, Farndon:** 01829 271242

FURTHER INFORMATION
- To view or print National Cycle Network routes, visit www.sustrans.org.uk
- Maps for this area are available to buy from www.sustransshop.co.uk
- **Nantwich Tourist Information:** 01270 537359
- **Chester Tourist Information:** 01244 351609; www.visitchester.com
- **Chester East Council:** www.cheshireeast.gov.uk

ROUTE DESCRIPTION
From Nantwich station, go straight into town by the Station Hotel to the pedestrianized town square, where you are faced with historic and half-timbered buildings on all sides. Look across the Green to St Mary's Church – the town's most ancient building. Go right down Pepper Street and turn left, then right to reach Nantwich Swimming Pool, one of the few saltwater open-air pools in the country. Here, pick up the riverside paths signed Regional Route 75. At the northern edge of the town, bear left on the shared footway until a toucan crossing over the main road takes you into a lovely route through the grounds of Reaseheath College (not a public right of way).

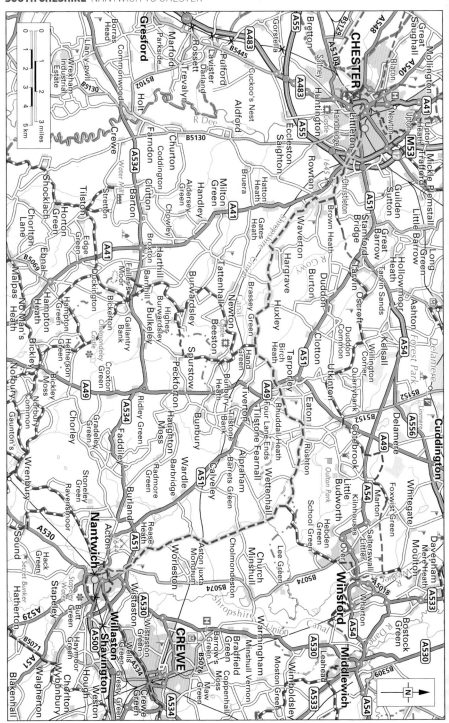

The ornate Eastgate Clock, Chester

Stained glass in Chester Cathedral

From here on, you are following generally quiet roads through very rural countryside. One mile after the village of Wettenhall, turn left on an unsigned route towards Townfield Farm and follow this road through Eaton, Tarporley and Huxley (now on National Route 45) on your way to Waverton. Join the towpath here, which is tarmac through Christleton to Chester.

Stay on the canal until you pass under the improbably named St Oswald's Way, or inner ring road, and then follow signs to the city centre, which you will reach via Eastgate under the clock built to celebrate Queen Victoria's Diamond Jubilee. The cathedral and town hall are just up Northgate to your right, or turn left for the river. If you want the train station, turn right over the canal just before the Mill Hotel (Egerton Street) and follow the signs through a traffic-calmed home zone to the station.

Chester is one of England's 18 Cycling Towns that are pursuing a range of initiatives and schemes to enhance and popularize cycling. This will ease access to the city centre, with planned two-way use for cyclists of all one-way streets. It is therefore possible that signed routes will evolve, so look out for the latest citywide cycle routes.

NEARBY CYCLE ROUTES

At Chester, the excellent Mickle Trafford to Dee Marsh Junction Railway Path offers a high-quality route to the north Wales coast (National Route 5). Regional Route 89 follows the River Dee path from the centre of Chester to Hawarden Bridge, where it meets National Route 5 (see page 14). National Route 56 goes north to Chester Zoo and through the Wirral to Birkenhead for the Mersey Ferry to Liverpool.

The circular Cheshire Cycleway (Regional Route 70) is 176 miles (283km) long and can be started from Chester.

The Pit and Dixon Cottages in Christleton

21

LIVERPOOL LOOPLINE – HALEWOOD TO AINTREE

This ride is part of the Trans Pennine Trail, which ends its route, from Hornsea on the North Sea coast, in Liverpool and Southport. Although this ride takes you only 10 miles (16km) to Aintree, Ride 4 in this book completes the Trail to Southport Promenade, 14 miles (22.5km) further on. Although this ride is entirely urban, it doesn't really feel so, as it takes the form of a woodland park either running through rocky cuttings or perched on high embankments with wide views over the city. It also links to a good number of open spaces, including the National Wildflower Centre at Court Hey Park, just south of the M62, and a little further north to Croxteth Hall & Country Park at West Derby, not to mention Aintree Racecourse, which is as famous a sporting ground as any in the country.

The Loopline was abandoned by the railways in 1964, and it was not until 1988 that Sustrans took on the task of rescuing the derelict route and turning it into the memorable local resource it is now. The Loopline's upkeep remains a considerable challenge and you may meet Sustrans maintenance rangers along the way, or one of a number of volunteer rangers who give their time freely to look after this route, and who will always welcome any support and assistance you can offer.

Racing in the Grand National at Aintree

ROUTE INFORMATION

National Route: 62
Start: Halewood train station.
Finish: Aintree train station.
Distance: 10 miles (16km).
Grade: Easy.
Surface: Tarmac.
Hills: None.

YOUNG & INEXPERIENCED CYCLISTS

This is an easy ride, almost entirely traffic-free.

REFRESHMENTS

- Lots of choice in Aintree and Halewood.

- The Metro Cafe Bar, Woolton.
- Halton Castle pub, West Derby.
- Stag & Rainbow pub, West Derby.
- The Coffee Jar, Broadway, Norris Green.

THINGS TO SEE & DO

- St Peter's Church, Woolton: where John Lennon and Paul McCartney first met in 1957, while waiting to play at the church dance, and the site of Eleanor Rigby's grave; www.stpeters-woolton.org.uk
- National Wildflower Centre, Court Hey Park, near Broad Green train station: seasonal wildflower demonstration areas, working

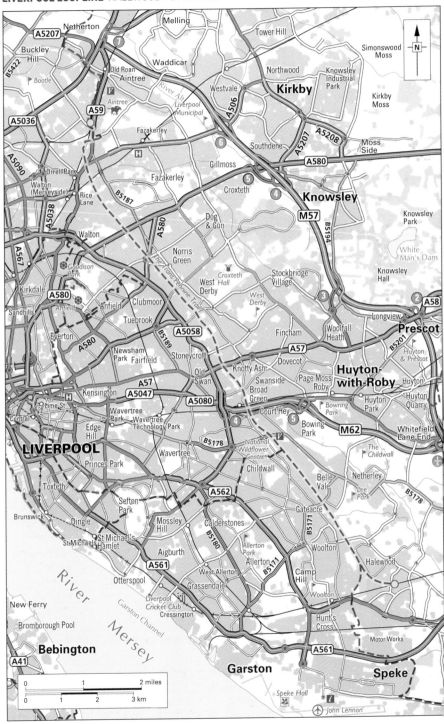

Croxteth Hall and Country Park

garden nursery, children's play area, exhibitions and cafe; 0151 738 1913; www.nwc.org.uk

- **Croxteth Hall & Country Park:** ancestral home of the Molyneux family, with historic hall, working farm, Victorian walled garden and 500-acre country park; 0151 233 6910; www.croxteth.co.uk
- **Aintree Racecourse:** home to the Grand National and other top meetings; 0151 523 2600; www.aintree.co.uk

TRAIN STATIONS
Halewood; Broad Green; Rice Lane; Aintree.

BIKE HIRE
- **Greenbank Cycle Hire, Greenbank Lane, Liverpool:** 0151 734 1296.
- **Liverpool Bicycle, Parliament Street, Liverpool:** 0151 707 6116; www.liverpool-bicycle.co.uk

FURTHER INFORMATION
- To view or print National Cycle Network routes, visit www.sustrans.org.uk
- Maps for this area are available to buy from www.sustransshop.co.uk and www.transpenninetrail.org.uk
- **Liverpool Tourist Information:** 0151 233 2008; www.visitliverpool.com

ROUTE DESCRIPTION
Starting at Halewood station in the south of Liverpool, cross straight over Hollies Road onto the railway path running up the eastern side of the Halewood Triangle. This area becomes a wide open space, managed by Knowsley Council as a country park, and you will soon join the main line of the Trans Pennine Trail coming in on the left from the Hunt's Cross direction.

From this point, the route runs on an embankment, with the path often cut into a ledge on one side or another in order to prevent the adjacent housing being overlooked.

At Well Lane, in Childwall, a route is signed to Liverpool Cathedral, and the Otterspool Promenade. Pier Head on the River Mersey is 7 miles (11km) away. Soon after, you go under the M62, very close to Broad Green station, and through Thomas Lane Tunnel, 80m (88 yards) long, to pass Sainsbury's supermarket at Knotty Ash. The route now enters 1.5 miles (2.5km) of railway cutting hewn out of the red sandstone of the area (the most famous example of this kind of cutting is between Edge Hill and Liverpool Lime Street on the original Manchester & Liverpool Railway). At the end of this stretch, you can turn off right at Mill Lane for a visit to Croxteth Hall & Country Park, or continue on high embankments and across a couple of large lattice bridges over Utting Avenue and Walton Hall Avenue, to reach Walton Hall Park and Rice Lane Recreation Ground (for a link to Rice Lane station).

The final section takes you under Walton Vale Shopping Centre to the mainline railway, to cross over the main road and link back to Aintree station. All the while, follow signs for the Trans Pennine Trail and National Route 62.

NEARBY CYCLE ROUTES
The Trans Pennine Trail (National Route 62) goes north to Southport (see page 26), and east to Runcorn and Warrington.

SEFTON COAST – AINTREE TO SOUTHPORT

A gentle ride from the home of the Grand National to the classic Victorian seaside resort of Southport. The route follows a section of the historic Leeds & Liverpool Canal, and several miles of the former Cheshire Lines railway, built to take people from the city to the seaside and providing extensive views across the Lancashire plain.

This route is the westernmost section of the Trans Pennine Trail, which starts at Hornsea on the east coast, then crosses the Pennines via the Woodhead Pass before coming through Manchester along the Mersey Valley. It finally reaches this level route across Downholland Moss, continuing to the sand dunes of Birkdale and Southport. Southport's beach and long pier are all within a few minutes of the end point of this ride, as are the Marine Lake and Victoria Park.

This route can easily be made into a circular one by following the towpath of the Leeds & Liverpool Canal at Crosby, and then picking up the coastal cycle route developed by Sefton Council through Hightown, Formby and Ainsdale. Merseyrail stations run closely parallel to the route, and there is a very frequent service along the coast to Southport.

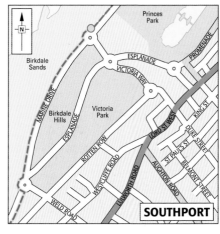

ROUTE INFORMATION
National Route: 62
Start: Aintree train station.
Finish: Sea Mark Sculpture, Marine Drive, Southport.
Distance: 15.5 miles (25km).
Grade: Easy.
Surface: Gravel track and tarmac paths.
Hills: One small very short hill before Maghull.

YOUNG & INEXPERIENCED CYCLISTS
Suitable for young families and novices, with four very short quiet road sections, connecting off-road paths, plus five main road crossings (three with cyclist-friendly toucan crossings).

REFRESHMENTS
- Shops and pubs in Aintree, Maghull, Ainsdale, Birkdale and Southport.
- Restaurant at Farmer Ted's Farm Park.

THINGS TO SEE & DO
- Farmer Ted's Farm Park, Flatmans Lane (B5195): interactive children's activity park

Marine Way Bridge, Southport

on a working farm; farm shop;
0151 526 0002; www.farmerteds.com
- Ainsdale Sand Dunes National Nature
Reserve, Ainsdale: home to some of the
best sand dune wildlife in Britain, with
red squirrels in the pine woodland;
01704 578774; www.seftoncoast.org.uk

Southport:
- New Pleasureland, Marine Drive:
amusement park, with over 60 rides and
attractions; 01704 532717
- British Lawnmower Museum, Shakespeare

Street: award-winning collection of garden
machinery; 01704 501336;
www.lawnmowerworld.com

TRAIN STATIONS
Aintree; Old Roan; Ainsdale; Hillside;
Birkdale; Southport.

BIKE HIRE
- Southport Eco Centre, Esplanade,
Southport: 0151 934 2711;
www.southportecocentre.com

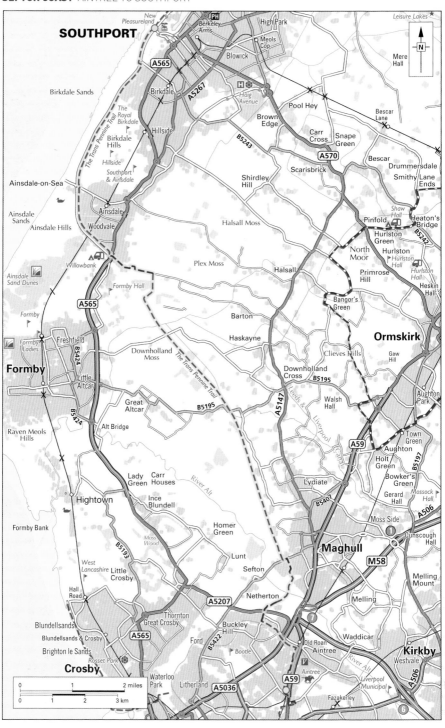

Ainsdale Sands,
Southport

Cyclist sculpture on
Southport Pier

FURTHER INFORMATION

- To view or print National Cycle Network routes, visit www.sustrans.org.uk
- Maps for this area are available to buy from www.sustransshop.co.uk and www.transpenninetrail.org.uk
- Southport Tourist Information: 01704 533333; www.visitsouthport.com

ROUTE DESCRIPTION

The station at Aintree stands in the shadow of the famous racecourse, with the grandstands towering over you as you leave the station. Turn right and wheel the few yards to reach the traffic lights. Here, turn right on the cyclepath that crosses the railway before turning right again to run parallel to the railway.

At the end of this, turn right and follow the road under the railway, then go left onto the minor road. After a few hundred metres (yards), this becomes an off-road path again, which takes you to a bridge over the Leeds & Liverpool Canal. Descend 'Wally's Steps' to the towpath – there is a cycle wheeling ramp on the right – and continue straight along the canal. A small swing bridge across the canal marks the point where you turn right and away from the waterside, following the minor road. Use the signalled crossing on Northern Perimeter Road

and continue straight ahead on Chapel Lane and then off-road again to Maghull.

Emerge onto Meadway, then go left into Old Racecourse Road, to reach the crossing on Sefton Lane. Here, turn left and go alongside the houses to reach the path along the old Cheshire Lines railway. For the next 7 miles (11km), you ride through green fields, with long views across the flat landscape. The first part of the line runs past the fields where the Waterloo Cup for hare coursing used to be staged.

Finally, the Trail bends right to Plex Moss Lane. Go left and follow this to the traffic lights. Cross the main road to the cyclepath. Soon sand dunes tower over you on Coastal Road. This section is close to the main road, so take the path a little to one side through the dunes and on into Southport to reach Marine Drive.

NEARBY CYCLE ROUTES

At Aintree, continue west on the Leeds & Liverpool Canal for Crosby and an excellent route northwards to Formby and the Ainsdale Nature Reserve. Alternatively, you could continue on the towpath and end up near Liverpool city centre. To the south, the Trans Pennine Trail continues along the Liverpool Loopline and then along the Mersey Valley to Manchester.

FALLOWFIELD LOOP – SOUTH MANCHESTER

The Fallowfield Loop is a particularly beautiful path constructed along a former railway that loops around the south side of Manchester. It passes under or over every road along the way, with the one exception of the Winslow Road, where a Sainsbury's supermarket blocks the route. The line was built by the Manchester, Sheffield & Lincolnshire Railway Company and opened in 1892. This is late in the history of the railways, giving the line many advantages: a generous amount of land was acquired, which made it more spacious; the bridges are nearly all contemporary and built in a similar style; and the company found it worthwhile to accommodate watercourses and aqueducts into the overall scheme. This all translates into a real urban park, albeit one that's 7 miles (11km) long. In addition, the line connects a number of other public spaces, including Chorlton Park in the west, Highfield Country Park, southeast of Levenshulme, and, towards the east, Debdale Park, with the two Gorton reservoirs. Chorlton Water Park is also close to the start point.

This whole route has been developed by Sustrans working with the support of the Friends of the Fallowfield Loop and in close cooperation with Manchester City Council, who have been responsible for strengthening many of the bridges you will pass along the way. The line is one of a number of former railways managed and maintained by Sustrans as part of its inventory of railways. These are being held for future railway use but put to good use in the meantime.

ROUTE INFORMATION
National Routes: 60, 6
Regional Route: 85
Start: Chorlton Park, Chorlton–cum–Hardy.
Finish: Fairfield train station, Manchester.
Distance: 6.5 miles (10.5km).
Grade: Easy.
Surface: Tarmac.
Hills: None.

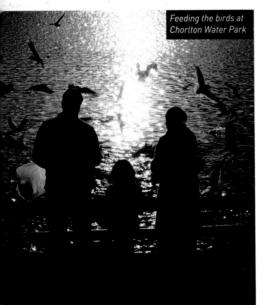
Feeding the birds at Chorlton Water Park

YOUNG & INEXPERIENCED CYCLISTS
The route is largely flat and traffic-free, making it well suited to young and inexperienced cyclists.

REFRESHMENTS
- Unicorn Grocery, organic and cooperative food shop, Albany Road, Chorlton.
- Lead Station restaurant, Beech Road, Chorlton.
- Lots of choice in Fallowfield area.
- Vale Cottage pub, Kirk Street, Gorton.
- The Bandstand pub, Hyde Road, by Debdale Park.

THINGS TO SEE & DO
- Chorlton Water Park: local nature reserve, with canoeing, angling and pond dipping;

Autumn at Chorlton Water Park

0161 881 5639; www.manchester.gov.uk
- **Highfield Country Park:** wooded wildlife haven; 0161 442 8324
- **Debdale Park:** based around the two Gorton reservoirs, with children's play areas, visitor centre and variety of wildlife; 0161 223 8278; www.manchester.gov.uk

TRAIN STATIONS
Fairfield.

BIKE HIRE
- Bicycle Boutique, All Saints, Manchester: 0161 273 7801; www.bicycleboutiquemcr.co.uk

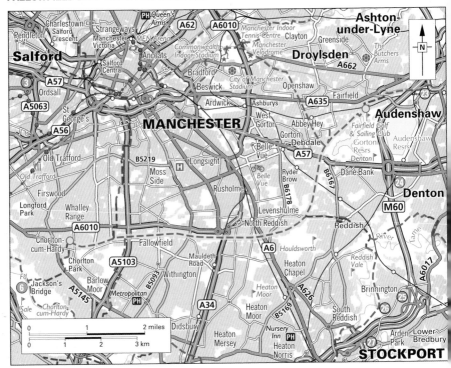

FURTHER INFORMATION

- To view or print National Cycle Network routes, visit www.sustrans.org.uk
- Maps for this area are available to buy from www.sustransshop.co.uk
- Fallowfield Loop: www.cycle-routes.org/fallowfieldloopline
- Cycling in Greater Manchester: www.cyclegm.org
- Manchester Tourist Information: 0871 222 8223; www.visitmanchester.com

ROUTE DESCRIPTION

The Fallowfield Loop route connects the River Mersey at Jackson's Bridge to the Ashton Canal just beyond Fairfield station.

A convenient point to start the ride is Chorlton Park, from where you follow National Route 60 signs to the railway path off the end of Sidbury Road. Note that the exact arrangement of route here will be revised while the metro is extended and a station reopened at Chorlton. A mile (1.6km) further

on, National Route 6, which is signed to Alexandra Park and the city centre, leads off into Athol Road on the left.

The path now runs east, with access points at intervals along the way until just after Wellington Street Bridge. Here, you take the ramp up to cycle along Sherwood Street and cross the busy Winslow Road at traffic lights. Turn left at this point for the universities. Once past Sainsbury's supermarket, the line runs through a wide cutting for 1.5 miles (2.5km), where considerable ingenuity in the construction of the line was needed to create a series of changing levels that would connect to adjacent roads and also avoid flooding.

Past the old Levenshulme station, the path runs up to go over the Fallowfield Brook (which itself went under the old railway via a siphon), and continues on a high embankment to look out over Manchester to the City Stadium. After crossing the Hyde Road on a high bridge, the route passes Gorton Lower Reservoir and links to the line of

Young herons in the Mersey Valley Country Park

he old Stockport Canal, which you could ollow left to join the Ashton Canal. Finally, at Abbey Hey, where the wide cuttings have een in-filled, the route with its wide-open paces loses all semblance of a railway and ends in a new section through recent housing at Fairfield station.

NEARBY CYCLE ROUTES

The Trans Pennine Trail (National Route 62) runs to the south of the Fallowfield Loop, through Stockport and the Mersey Valley, while Route 6 runs north through the city centre and on to Bury.

ROTHER VALLEY RIDE

Rother Valley is a vast 750-acre award-winning country park created on a former opencast mine on the edge of Sheffield. It is home to water sports, including cable water-skiing, sailing and canoeing, and you can also hire bikes and play a round of golf. There are miles of paths to be explored and many quieter areas where you can enjoy the wildlife. At its centre is an historic mill building, which is home to a visitor centre and cafe.

Poolsbrook is a newer 180-acre country park on the site of another former colliery, which now boasts woodland, grassland and water habitats, abundant with wildlife.

The route between these two country parks follows the old railway south to Staveley and on to Poolsbrook. This is part of the former Grand Central Main Line opened in 1899 and closed in 1966.

ROUTE INFORMATION

National Route: 67
Start: Visitor centre, Rother Valley Country Park.
Finish: Visitor centre, Poolsbrook Country Park.
Distance: 7 miles (11km).
Grade: Easy.
Surface: Gravel track.
Hills: None.

YOUNG & INEXPERIENCED CYCLISTS

Off-road all the way, with a few vehicles sharing a short section of the route in Rother Valley Country Park.

REFRESHMENTS

- Cafe at Rother Valley Country Park.
- Sitwell Arms Hotel, Renishaw.
- Cafe at Poolsbrook Country Park.

THINGS TO SEE & DO

- **Rother Valley Country Park:** wide range of activities and facilities; 0114 247 1452; www.rothervalley.f9.co.uk
- **Poolsbrook Country Park:** wildlife, children's adventure play area, picnic sites and more; 01246 470579; www.poolsbrookcountrypark.org.uk

TRAIN STATIONS

Chesterfield is 4.5 miles (7km) from Poolsbrook Country Park along a signed section of the Trans Pennine Trail cycle route (part on-road, part traffic-free), via Brimington Common.

BIKE HIRE

- **Watersports Centre, Rother Valley Country Park:** 0114 247 1452; www.rothervalley.f9.co.uk

FURTHER INFORMATION

- To view or print National Cycle Network routes, visit www.sustrans.org.uk
- Maps for this area are available to buy from www.sustransshop.co.uk
- **Trans Pennine Trail:** www.transpenninetrail.org.uk
- **Chesterfield Tourist Information:** 01246 345777; www.visitchesterfield.info

ROUTE DESCRIPTION

From the visitor centre at Rother Valley Country Park, follow the roadway leading south. Pass the Watersports Centre and, as the road leads to the water-ski centre, go straight on through the gates onto the well-surfaced path that leads all the way around the lake. On the far side of the lake, turn left by the Trail information board to go under the railway and out of the park. Turn left again to join the start of the old railway. Heading almost due south, you now quickly cross over the River Rother and pass the former Killamarsh station on your way to Renishaw. Here, you slope down to a car

Sailing at the Rother Valley
Country Park

park and straight back up to rejoin the line of the old railway.

To the left is a (very) short section of reinstated canal. This is currently isolated but part of a grand plan to slowly restore the whole 46 miles (74km) of the Chesterfield Canal. The canal was built on the route mapped out by the famous canal engineer James Brindley to connect the River Rother at Chesterfield to the River Trent and beyond. The canal fully opened in 1777.

Just north of Staveley, the route bends right, then left, to access a bridge over the live railway. Immediately after this, there is a

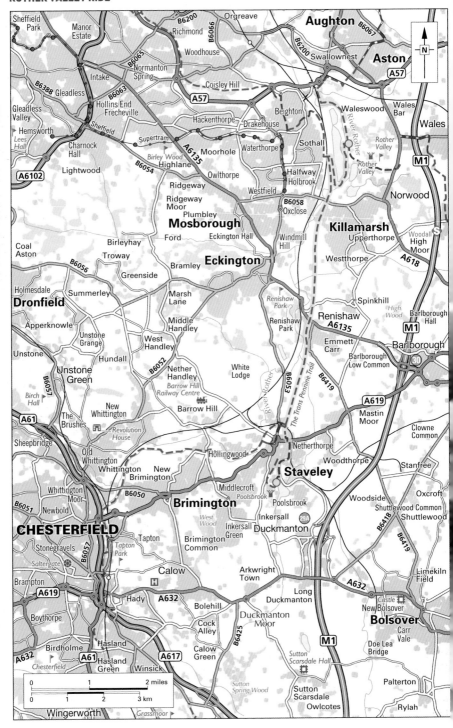

Rother Valley Country Park visitor centre

junction where the Trans Pennine Trail route splits – you go straight on, along the old railway. Passing through Staveley, two bridges carry the route over roads. Just before the second of these bridges (over Inkersall Road), turn off to the left and follow the path that leads into Poolsbrook Country Park and up to the cafe and visitor centre.

NEARBY CYCLE ROUTES

This route is on the southern part of the Trans Pennine Trail, which runs between Leeds and Chesterfield (National Route 67), and Southport and Hornsea (Routes 62 and 65).

From Rother Valley, Route 6 heads north to Rotherham and east to Worksop. Route 67 runs northwest to Sheffield and on to Barnsley.

At Staveley, the Trans Pennine Trail splits, with both routes eventually reaching Chesterfield. From Poolsbrook Country Park, the route continues along the old railway to Inkersall Green. From here, a combination of bridleways and quiet lanes takes a winding route through to Chesterfield station, 4.5 miles (7km) away.

Alternatively, from just north of Staveley, a cycle route follows the Chesterfield Canal towpath all the way to the visitor centre at

Autumn in Poolsbrook Country Park

Tapton Lock on the outskirts of Chesterfield. A further section of the Trans Pennine Trail provides a link to Chesterfield station, 4.5 miles (7km) away, mostly via towpath.

UPPER DON VALLEY – WORTLEY TO DUNFORD BRIDGE

This scenic ride runs through the foothills of the South Yorkshire Pennines to Dunford Bridge, a remote hamlet on the edge of the Peak District National Park. However, as it follows the old Woodhead railway line, it remains easy going all the way. You'll go through the old railway tunnel at Thurgoland, through the attractive market town of Penistone and out to Dunford Bridge, lying beneath the Winscar Reservoir. Water draining down from the moorland around Grains Moss forms small rivers that join together to form the source of the River Don, which feeds into the reservoir. This is a popular route in a beautiful and historic landscape, well used by walkers and horse riders as well as cyclists.

The railway line first opened in 1845 between Manchester and Sheffield. The line was electrified in 1954, with the completion of a third Woodhead tunnel through the Pennines at Dunford Bridge. The railway closed completely in 1981 and the route converted to the Trans Pennine Trail on either side of the tunnel. The tunnels now carry National Grid's high-voltage cables through the Pennines.

A treasure hunt is available for the Penistone to Dunford Bridge section of this ride (www.transpenninetrail.org.uk).

Cattle crossing the River Don

ROUTE INFORMATION
National Routes: 62, 6
Start: Cote Green Lane car park, Wortley.
Finish: Dunford Bridge car park.
Distance: 9.5 miles (16km). Shorter options: from Penistone to Dunford Bridge 6 miles (10km); from Wortley to Penistone 4 miles (6.5km).
Grade: Easy.
Surface: Gravel tracks, with a few short tarmac sections at Penistone and Thurgoland.
Hills: None.

YOUNG & INEXPERIENCED CYCLISTS
No on-road sections or busy roads to cross. Although the route can be started at either end, cycling from Wortley to Dunford Bridge means the return trip is downhill.

REFRESHMENTS
- Pennine Equine, at the car park in Wortley, has a shop selling ice cream.
- Pubs in Thurgoland, Oxspring and Millhouse Green – all just off the route.
- Various choices in Penistone.

THINGS TO SEE & DO

- **Wortley Top Forge Industrial Museum, Thurgoland:** the oldest surviving heavy iron forge in the world; 0114 288 7576; www.topforge.co.uk
- **Peak District National Park:** Britain's first national park, established in1951; www.peakdistrict.org

TRAIN STATIONS

Penistone.

BIKE HIRE

None locally.

FURTHER INFORMATION

- To view or print National Cycle Network routes, visit www.sustrans.org.uk
- Maps for this area are available to buy from www.sustransshop.co.uk
- **Trans Pennine Trail:** www.transpenninetrail.org.uk
- **Penistone Tourist Information:** www.visitpenistone.co.uk

ROUTE DESCRIPTION

From the Cote Green Lane car park at Wortley, go down the slope onto the old railway line, turning right and heading into the cutting

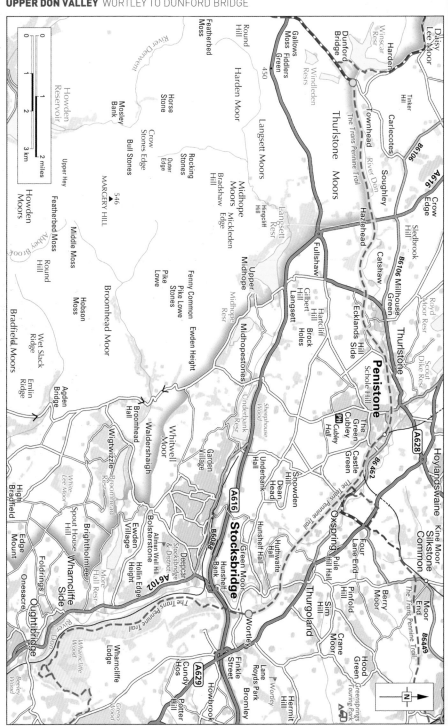

Royd Moor Wind Farm, Penistone

towards Penistone. After about a mile (1.6km), you come to the 300m (329-yard) long Thurgoland tunnel. This curves, which means you can't see the far end as you enter, but the tunnel is lit from 6am to midnight every day, although on a bright day the lights can seem a little dim. An alternative route on quiet lanes is signed before you reach the tunnel.

Immediately after the tunnel, you can enjoy views from the viaduct that carries you over the River Don before the landscape opens out around you. Continue along the old railway through Oxspring and you soon arrive in Penistone, where there is direct access to the train station from the route and an off-road route through the town. To detour into town, local signs take you on-road into the centre from several points. To rejoin the trail, either retrace your steps or follow signs leading back to the route by the recreation ground and park.

From here the route heads west. There are a couple of quiet lanes to cross, but new bridges take you over two busy roads. As the hills rise around you, look for the wind farm at Royd Moor. A brown sign leads up to the viewpoint.

The Peak District moors come into view as you pass the old station at Hazlehead, and soon you arrive at the 'end of the line' in Dunford Bridge. The old railway tunnels that cut through

A lit tunnel on the Trans Pennine Trail

the Pennines for 3 miles (5km) can be seen from the road bridge over the old railway.

NEARBY CYCLE ROUTES

This route is part of the Trans Pennine Trail (National Routes 62 and 65), running between Southport and Hornsea, and Leeds and Chesterfield (Route 67). This continues west from Dunford Bridge through the Woodhead Pass, while from Oxspring and Wortley there are mainly off-road routes eastwards into the Dearne Valley, and from Wortley there are routes to Sheffield and Rotherham.

The Pennine Cycleway (Route 68) follows the Trans Pennine Trail over the Pennines and north to Holmfirth, west of Dunford Bridge.

PENDLE COUNTRY – FOULRIDGE TO GARGRAVE

The area of Lancashire known as Pendle is at the eastern edge of the county, bordering on the Yorkshire Dales and the Pennine hills. Pendle takes its name from Pendle Hill, which, at 558m (1,831ft) high, dominates the skyline of the area. The Leeds & Liverpool Canal links Foulridge (north of Colne) in Lancashire with Gargrave in Yorkshire, via stone-built villages and the ancient market town of Barnoldswick. Known locally as Barlick, this is the highest town on what is the longest canal in Britain. This ride parts company with the canal after a while but keeps you on the Pennine Cycleway (one of the longest cycle routes in Britain) to the picturesque village of Gargrave on the edge of the Dales, where the canal, the famous Leeds–Settle–Carlisle Railway and Pennine Way National Trail all pass through. It also sits astride the River Aire, only 7 miles (11km) from its source near Malham Cove.

There's some lovely scenery throughout, and you might be lucky and catch sight of a kingfisher darting about the canal. For a small donation, you can see the stalactites and stalagmites in the cellars of the Anchor Inn at Salterforth. Greenberfield Locks, just beyond Barnoldswick, is the highest point on the Leeds & Liverpool Canal.

Note that cycling permits are required on British Waterways-owned canal towpaths. Download one free of charge from www.waterscape.com or call their customer services team on 0845 671 5530.

ROUTE INFORMATION

National Route: 68 (Pennine Cycleway)
Start: Foulridge Wharf, Foulridge.
Finish: Gargrave village.

Distance: 11 miles (17.3km). Shorter option: from Foulridge Wharf to Greenberfield Locks 4 miles (6.5km).
Grade: Medium.

Boats at the lock near Gargrave

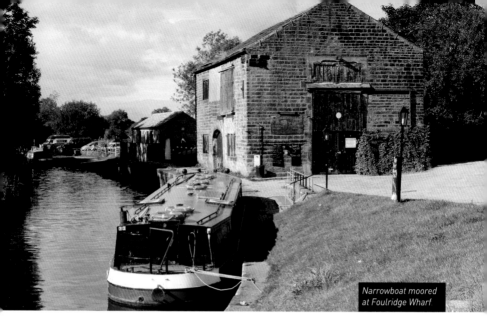

Narrowboat moored at Foulridge Wharf.

Surface: Good towpath, with just a few cobbles in places, uneven stones under bridges and puddles when wet. Tarmac on-road section.
Hills: One small hill to climb over and descend after West Marton.

YOUNG & INEXPERIENCED CYCLISTS

Foulridge Wharf to Greenberfield Locks is traffic-free and flat, making it ideal for young

and inexperienced cyclists. Bear in mind that on the canal towpath cyclists give way to other users (part of the Waterways Code). The road section from Bridge 159 beyond Greenberfield Locks to Gargrave undulates with one steep descent, and unaccompanied children should not attempt the crossing of the A59 at West Marton, which has fast-moving traffic.

REFRESHMENTS

- Cafe Cargo, Foulridge Wharf.
- Anchor Inn, Salterforth.
- Choice in Barnoldswick.
- Lock Stop snack bar, Greenberfield Locks.
- West Marton Lodge Tea Room (left onto the busy A59 at the village crossroads).
- Masons Arms pub, Gargrave.
- The Dalesman Cafe, Gargrave.

THINGS TO SEE & DO

- Bancroft Mill, Barnoldswick: restored cotton weaving mill with demonstrations (limited weekend and seasonal opening); 01282 865626
- St Andrew's Parish Church, Gargrave: stained-glass windows dating from 1852; the tower escaped the Scots raid of 1318.
- Pendle Heritage Centre, Barrowford: museum, art gallery, 18th-century walled

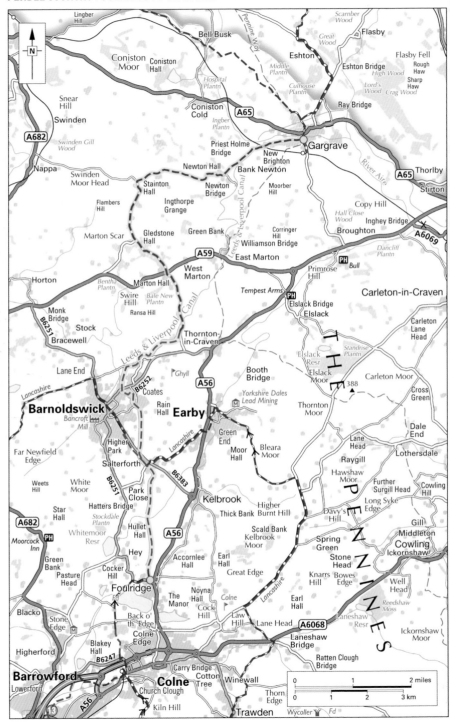

Ancient track along Pendle Hill

garden, cruck barn, farmyard animals and tearoom; 01282 661702; www.htnw.co.uk

TRAIN STATIONS
Gargrave.

BIKE HIRE
- Dave Ferguson Cycles, Skipton: 01756 795367

Canalside cycling near Salterforth

FURTHER INFORMATION
- To view or print National Cycle Network routes, visit www.sustrans.org.uk
- Maps for this area are available to buy from www.sustransshop.co.uk
- Barnoldswick Tourist Information: 01282 666704
- Yorkshire Dales Tourist Information: www.yorkshiredales.org.uk
- Cycling Lancashire: 01772 530201; www.lancashire.gov.uk/cycling

ROUTE DESCRIPTION
From Foulridge Wharf, follow the canal towpath northwards to Salterforth, Barnoldswick and Greenberfield Locks. About a mile (1.6km) further, go under Bridge 159, bear right up onto the road and turn right. At West Marton, take care crossing the busy A59. Climb the hill and descend to pass Stainton Hall. Bear right at the fork in the road for Bank Newton and Gargrave. Cross over the Leeds & Liverpool Canal again just before going underneath the Leeds–Settle–Carlisle Railway line. On reaching Gargrave, turn left by the pub and cross the River Aire. You'll see blue signs for Route 68 all the way.

NEARBY CYCLE ROUTES
The Pennine Cycleway (National Route 68) continues south from Foulridge, through Colne and Nelson, to the Peak District and Derby. North from Gargrave, the route goes through the western Dales to Berwick-upon-Tweed. See the 8-mile (13km) circular family-friendly route from Gargrave at www.cyclethedales.org.uk or the 260-mile (418km) Lancashire Cycleway (Regional Route 91).

OLD MOOR NATURE RESERVE TO SPROTBROUGH

Once dominated by the coal-mining industry, the Dearne Valley has changed beyond all recognition in the last 20 years. The area is now a green and pleasant land as reclamation schemes have created and enhanced nature reserves, wetland habitats and riverside paths through the valley. This ride explores this landscape, following the River Dearne from the very popular RSPB Old Moor nature reserve through to Sprotbrough in the Don Gorge. While the river may look tranquil, it is not always so. In June 2007, torrential rain swelled the river, which rose several feet above the level of the path at Old Moor, completely washing it away, as well as the wooden bridge that you cross over.

Sir Walter Scott wrote his novel *Ivanhoe* at The Boat Inn at Sprotbrough, inspired by 12th-century Conisbrough Castle standing guard over the valley towards the end of the route. Built of magnesian limestone, the castle is the only example of its kind in Europe.

ROUTE INFORMATION

National Route: 62
Start: RSPB Old Moor nature reserve.
Finish: Sprotbrough Lock.
Distance: 10 miles (16km).
Grade: Easy.
Surface: Mainly gravel tracks and a few sections of tarmac path and one short tarmac road section. The path alongside the River Don will be muddy after occasional flooding.
Hills: None.

YOUNG & INEXPERIENCED CYCLISTS

There are three road crossings on the route. The second, by the rail viaduct, needs extra care. There is a short on-road section at Harlington village, most of which has a 30mph (48km/h) limit. A section of this can be avoided by a slightly longer off-road detour.

Conisbrough Castle

OLD MOOR NATURE RESERVE TO SPROTBROUGH

REFRESHMENTS
- Cafe at the RSPB Old Moor nature reserve.
- Pub and village shop in Harlington.
- Boat Inn on the riverside at Sprotbrough.

THINGS TO SEE & DO
- **RSPB Old Moor nature reserve:** teeming with birds throughout the year; 01226 751593; www.rspb.org.uk
- **Conisbrough Castle:** 1 mile (1.6km) off the route: fine example of Norman military architecture, with its white cylindrical keep offering far-reaching views; 01709 863329; www.english-heritage.org.uk/conisbrough

TRAIN STATIONS
Bolton-Upon-Dearne; Conisbrough.

BIKE HIRE
None locally.

FURTHER INFORMATION
- To view or print National Cycle Network routes, visit www.sustrans.org.uk
- Maps for this area are available to buy from www.sustransshop.co.uk
- Trans Pennine Trail: www.transpenninetrail.org.uk
- Doncaster Tourist Information: 01302 734309; www.visitdoncaster.co.uk

ROUTE DESCRIPTION
From the RSPB Old Moor nature reserve car park, exit the bridge over the stream to access the Trans Pennine Trail. Make sure you take time to explore the award-winning reserve before you set off or on your return. The information board in front of you tells you more about the area and your route. Head left along the well-surfaced path, which will take you under the car park access road. Where the path forks, take the track to the left up the short slope. The path levels out and there are views across the RSPB wetlands as you head towards the River Dearne.

Cyclists dwarfed by the viaduct at Conisbrough

Follow the riverside until you cross a wooden bridge. The path on the other side goes through woodland before reaching the road. Cross at the lights and continue on the obvious path. This leads through the most recently reclaimed site in the valley, where a staggering 66,000 trees have been planted as part of the restoration project. Take particular care at the second road crossing at the end of this site before you pass through the railway arch. A tarmac off-road route takes you through to Adwick Bridge.

Cross the river and head straight on, past the parking area and over the lane. Follow the path that curves right before turning right onto a quiet lane. Turn right at the end of the lane and then next left into Harlington village. Continue through the village, turning right into Mill Lane. This will take you back down to the riverside. Here, go left onto the flood bank to reach

Adult male lapwing at Old Moor reserve

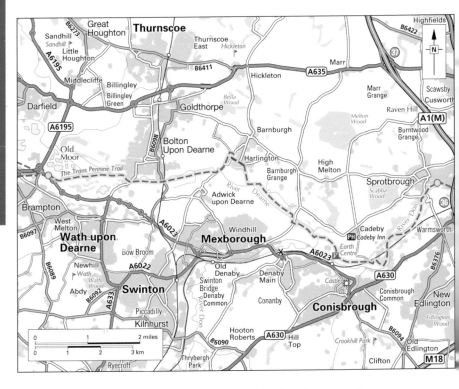

Pastures Road. Cross the river and then the road to follow the obvious path straight ahead, bridging the River Dearne for a final time before a climb up that brings Conisbrough Castle into view. Just before the old rail viaduct, turn off left and snake down to the foot of the viaduct, where the route turns to follow the River Don. Following the river, but with a woodland feel, the path leads through the scenic Don Gorge to the Boat Inn and lock at Sprotbrough.

NEARBY CYCLE ROUTES

This route is part of the Trans Pennine Trail (National Routes 62 and 65), which runs between Southport and Hornsea, and Leeds to Chesterfield (Route 67). This continues west to Penistone via Worsbrough, or there is an alternative route via Elsecar. The Trail to the east coast continues along the riverside beyond Sprotbrough Lock before turning north to Bentley and, eventually, Selby.

Around Conisbrough Castle

BIRKBY BRADLEY, CALDER VALLEY & SPEN VALLEY GREENWAYS

Linking Huddersfield and Bradford city centres and Dewsbury town centre, this mainly traffic-free route is ideal for family leisure cycling. Much of it is surprisingly rural, passing through a pleasant wooded and agricultural landscape. Most of the path is built on the former rail corridor of the Midland Railway, with the section from Dewsbury Moor to the town centre on a riverside path. It comprises the Birkby Bradley Greenway (National Route 69) and Calder Valley Greenway (National Route 66). At Dewsbury Moor, the Calder Valley Greenway joins the Spen Valley, which runs north through Heckmondwike, Liversedge and Cleckheaton.

There are many scenic views along the way, including those from Riddings woodland across Huddersfield to Huddersfield Football Stadium and Dalton Bank, and from Lower Spen up the Spen Valley to Norristhorpe and Roberttown. Other points of interest include Bradley Viaduct, which carries you over the River Colne and Huddersfield Broad Canal, and the River Calder bridge across the Dewsbury flood alleviation channel, with an excellent view of the river and weir. There are also local nature reserves at Dalton Bank and Lower Spen.

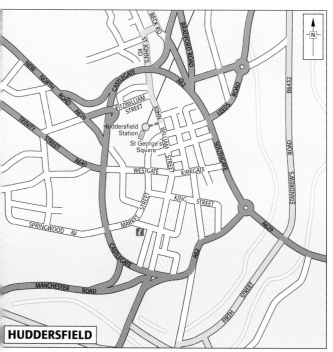

ROUTE INFORMATION

National Routes: 69, 66

Start: Huddersfield train station.

Finish: Bradford Centenary Square. For a shorter option, finish the ride at Dewsbury train station.

Distance: Huddersfield to Bradford 18 miles (29km); Huddersfield to Dewsbury 9 miles (14.5km).

Grade: Easy to moderate.

Surface: Tarmac.

Hills: Some moderate inclines on the Birkby Bradley and Calder Valley Greenways; a gentle climb from Dewsbury to

View of Bradford from National Media Museum

Harold Wilson statue, Huddersfield station

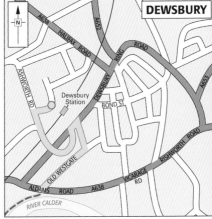

DEWSBURY

Oakenshaw; and a few moderate climbs from the Spen Valley Greenway into Bradford.

YOUNG & INEXPERIENCED CYCLISTS

Birkby Bradley and Calder Valley Greenways: there are some short on-road sections, mostly on quiet roads. You will need to cross the busy A62 Leeds Road at Bradley using the central refuge islands provided. There is also a short but busy road section with cycle lanes out of Mirfield.

Spen Valley Greenway: there is one busy road with a signalized crossing at the southern end as you arrive in the centre of Dewsbury. Best for novices and families is the 7-mile (11km) section from the Calder & Hebble Navigation north to Oakenshaw. There are several roads to negotiate between the end of the Spen Valley

Greenway in Oakenshaw and Bradford centre but the route into the city mainly follows off-road sections and on-road cycle lanes.

REFRESHMENTS

- Lots of choice in Huddersfield, Mirfield, Dewsbury, Heckmondwike, Cleckheaton and Bradford, although these will require a short detour from the route.

THINGS TO SEE & DO
Huddersfield:
- Castle Hill and Victoria Tower: built to

*Good Samaritan
statue, Dewsbury*

arrangement;
www.dewsbury
busmuseum.co.uk
• **Dewsbury
Museum:** exhibits
focusing on
childhood;
01924 325100;
www.kirklees.gov.uk

commemorate Queen Victoria's Diamond
Jubilee; 01484 223830; www.kirklees.gov.uk
• **Tolson Museum:** Victorian mansion house
with a varied collection; 01484 223830;
www.kirklees.gov.uk
• **Bradley Viaduct:** spectacular blue brick
viaduct, with 15 high arches over the River
Colne and Huddersfield Broad Canal.

Dewsbury:
• Victorian buildings, many connected with the
once-thriving textiles trade.
• **Oakwell Hall:** Elizabethan house, which
Charlotte Brontë visited in the 19th century
and featured in her novel *Shirley*;
01924 326240; www.kirklees.gov.uk
• **Red House Museum:** elegant Georgian home
of the Taylor family, friends of Charlotte
Brontë; 01274 335100; www.kirklees.gov.uk
• **Dewsbury Bus Museum:** vintage buses, with
open days twice a year and other visits by

• **The Minster:** Dewsbury's historic parish
church dating from AD 627;
www.dewsburyminster.org.uk

Bradford:
• **Bradford Cathedral:** dating from the 15th
century; www.bradfordcathedral.co.uk
• **National Media Museum:** focusing on film,
photography, television, radio and the web;
0844 856 3797;
www.nationalmediamuseum.org.uk
• **Bradford Industrial Museum:** permanent
displays of textile machinery, steam power,
engineering and motor vehicles;
01274 435900; www.bradfordmuseums.org
• **Cartwright Hall Art Gallery:** civic art gallery
with contemporary exhibitions and
permanent collections; 01274 431212;
www.bradfordmuseums.org
• **Spen Valley:** public artworks line the route,
including Sally Matthews' *Swaledale sheep*.

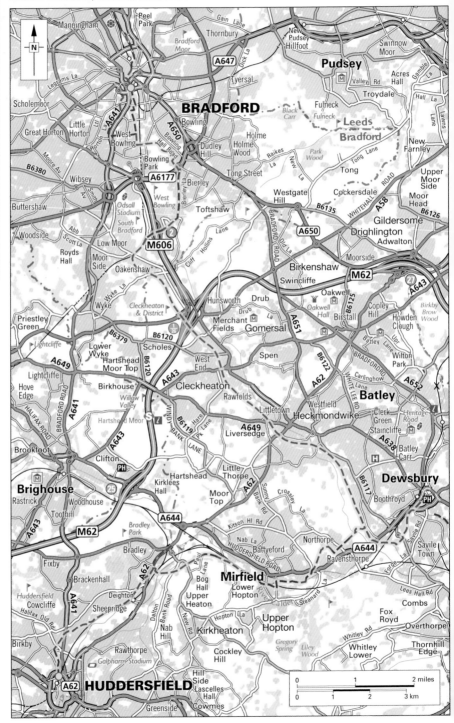

'Swaledale Sheep' by
Sally Matthews

'Cycle Seats' by
Alan Evans

'Broad Bottom Gorillas'
near Broadbottom Lock

TRAIN STATIONS

Huddersfield; Deighton; Mirfield; Ravensthorpe;
Dewsbury; Bradford.

BIKE HIRE

Enquire locally.

FURTHER INFORMATION

- To view or print National Cycle Network
  routes, visit www.sustrans.org.uk
- Maps for this area are available to buy from
  www.sustransshop.co.uk
- **Huddersfield Tourist Information:**
  01484 223200; www.kirklees.gov.uk
- **Bradford Tourist Information:** 01274 433678;
  www.visitbradford.com

ROUTE DESCRIPTION

From the new civic square in Huddersfield,
outside the magnificent porticoed train station,
follow, on-road, the National Route 69 signs
to the railway path. Continue on the greenway
through the Colne Valley, following the course
of the Huddersfield Broad Canal. Cross the
busy Leeds Road to join National Route 66 and
the Calder Valley Greenway. You will go over the
splendid Bradley Viaduct, crossing the canal
and River Colne. Between Colne Bridge and
Mirfield train station, there are quiet roads with

traffic-free sections. From Mirfield station,
cross the canal and take the short, busy road
section with cycle lanes towards Ravensthorpe.
There is a traffic-free section on the edge of the
town before you reach Sackville Street and a
traffic-free link to the Spen Valley Greenway.

Here, either cycle south on traffic-free paths
that, for a short distance, go alongside the River
Calder before taking you into Dewsbury, or go
north, on a gentle traffic-free ascent seemingly
over the top of Heckmondwike, Liversedge and
Cleckheaton before passing through a rolling
golf course to the Spen Valley's end at
Oakenshaw. From Oakenshaw, take the
signposted route along cycle lanes and paths
under the M606 to Bierley, through Bowling
Park and on to Bradford Centenary Square.

NEARBY CYCLE ROUTES

National Route 66 runs from Leeds, northwest
to Shipley, then south through Bradford to
Dewsbury before turning west again along the
Calder Valley. There are two long traffic-free
trails out of Leeds: the Leeds & Liverpool Canal
northwest to Shipley, Bingley and Keighley (see
page 54), and the Aire & Calder Navigation
southeast to Woodlesford. Further south, there
are many traffic-free sections of the Trans
Pennine Trail close to Barnsley.

AIRE VALLEY TOWPATH – LEEDS TO BINGLEY

At approximately 127 miles (204km) long, the Leeds & Liverpool Canal is Britain's longest canal. The section alongside the River Aire between Leeds city centre and Bingley is full of historical interest and some surprisingly scenic countryside. The canal winds its way out of vibrant Leeds, past the parkland setting of medieval Kirkstall Abbey and picturesque havens like Bramley Falls and Rodley Nature Reserve. Leeds Industrial Museum is located at Armley Mills, between the Leeds & Liverpool Canal and the River Aire at Armley (Bridge 225). The village of Saltaire, a UNESCO World Heritage Site, is just beyond Shipley and provides a definite highlight of the journey, with its magnificent Italianate mill that is now home to the largest collection of David Hockney paintings in Britain.

Finally Bingley, the home of the world-famous Five Rise Locks and its equally impressive neighbour, the Three Rise Locks. Both are magnificent examples of engineering and design and great places to pause for a while and watch the boats pass through.

Note that cycling permits are required on British Waterways-owned canal towpaths. Download one free of charge from www.waterscape.com or call their customer services team on 0845 671 5530.

ROUTE INFORMATION
National Routes: 66, 69
Start: Office Lock Bridge on Canal Wharf (off Water Lane), Leeds.
Finish: Five Rise Locks swing bridge.

Distance: 13 miles (21km). Shorter option: from Office Lock Bridge to Rodley 6.5 miles (10.5km).
Grade: Easy.
Surface: Mostly good with some tarmac.
Hills: None.

Saltaire is a UNESCO World Heritage Site

YOUNG & INEXPERIENCED CYCLISTS
This is an ideal ride for young and novice cyclists, as it's all traffic-free and largely level,

Young cyclist at Dowley Gap

Exhibit at the Royal Armouries Museum

except for the short climb to the top of Five Rise Locks; watch your speed on the descent and remember that pedestrians have priority over cyclists on the towpath. The Waterways Code can be read on boards along the way. Take care at the busy road crossing at Apperley Bridge.

REFRESHMENTS

- Cafes, pubs and restaurants around Water Lane and Bridgewater Place, Leeds.
- Old Bridge Inn, Kirkstall.
- The Abbey Inn, Pollard Lane, near Fallwood Marina.

- Cafe and pubs at Rodley.
- Cafe and pubs at Apperley Bridge.
- Choice in Shipley town centre.
- Cafes in Saltaire.
- Cafe and diner at Salt's Mill, Saltaire.
- The Fisherman's pub, Dowley Gap.
- Choice in Bingley, including Five Rise Locks Cafe.

THINGS TO SEE & DO

- **Royal Armouries Museum, Leeds:** purpose-built to house the arms and armour collection from the Tower of London; 0113 220 1999; www.royalarmouries.org
- **Leeds Industrial Museum, Armley Mills, Leeds:** one of the largest textile museums in the world; 0113 263 7861; www.leeds.gov.uk/armleymills

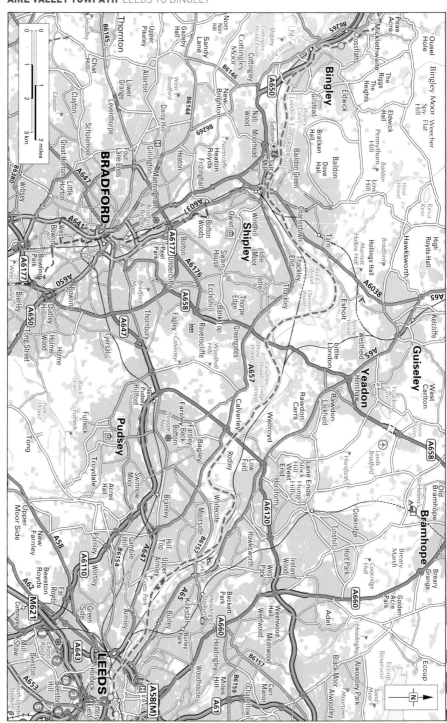

Cycling by Bingley
Five Rise Locks

- **Kirkstall Abbey:** one of the best-preserved Cistercian monasteries in the country; 0113 230 5492; www.leeds.gov.uk/kirkstallabbey
- **Saltaire World Heritage Site:** Victorian industrial village; home to the Salt's Mill art galleries; 01274 531163; www.saltsmill.org.uk; www.visitbradford.com
- **Five Rise Locks, Bingley:** opened in 1774 and the most spectacular feature of the Leeds & Liverpool Canal.

TRAIN STATIONS
Leeds; Shipley; Saltaire; Bingley.

BIKE HIRE
None locally.

FURTHER INFORMATION
- To view or print National Cycle Network routes, visit www.sustrans.org.uk
- Maps for this area are available to buy from www.sustransshop.co.uk
- **Leeds Tourist Information:** 0113 242 5242; www.visitleeds.co.uk
- **Aire Valley Towpath:** www.airevalleytowpath.org.uk
- **Bradford Tourist Information:** 01274 433678 www.visitbradford.com

ROUTE DESCRIPTION
From Office Lock Bridge in Leeds, simply follow the clearly signposted route along the canal towpath all the way to Bingley. After Shipley, the route is known as the Airedale Greenway, and the route number changes from 66 to 69.

NEARBY CYCLE ROUTES
Continuing along the towpath from Five Rise Locks at Bingley brings you to open countryside again. At the fourth bridge from the locks you can join Granby Lane and visit East Riddlesden Hall (National Trust), a 17th-century West Riding manor house with gardens and tearoom.

Further along National Route 69 at Silsden, the West Yorkshire Cycle Route can be joined but it's a challenging 150-mile (241km) circuit.

The section of the Leeds & Liverpool Canal that runs from Shipley to Bingley also forms part of the Airedale Greenway, a local route in Airedale that connects the three main towns of Shipley, Bingley and Keighley. From Shipley, you can also cycle on through Bradford, following an on-road route that connects to the Spen Valley Greenway (see page 49).

YORK TO SELBY & BENINGBROUGH HALL

This pleasant 25-mile (40km) ride is composed of two mostly traffic-free routes running north and south from the beautiful walled city of York. They can be ridden separately or as one continuous trip from one of three different start points. Each route takes you through Yorkshire's capital city, famous for its Roman and Viking connections.

The ride to the north runs parallel with the broad, slow-moving River Ouse and follows a traffic-free path before joining quiet lanes through the little villages of Overton and Shipton. Beningbrough Hall is a superb 18th-century mansion, park and gardens which gives a view of life in an English country house from Georgian to Victorian times.

Heading south from York towards Selby, the route runs across the flat, arable landscape of the Vale of York to Riccall and then on to Selby. The ride uses the former East Coast mainline threatened by subsidence during development of the huge Selby coalfield. It was bought by Sustrans for £1 and converted to a cycling and walking route in one of their very first projects. It includes the famous artwork of the solar system built at a scale of 575,872,239 to 1. With every 100 metres along the track corresponding to more than 57 million kilometres in space, it's easy to cycle at 10 times the speed of light, which means every journey down the route ends before it begins, and each time you travel on it you will become a little younger.

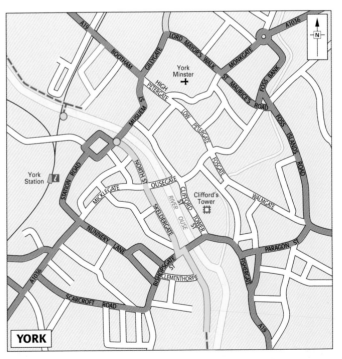

ROUTE INFORMATION

National Route: 65
Start and Finish: York Station, Selby Station, Beningbrough Hall.
Distance: York to Selby 15 miles (24km); York to Beningbrough 10 miles (16km). Total route: Selby to Beningbrough 25 miles (40km).
Grade: Easy.
Surface: Tarmac cyclepaths and quiet lanes.
Hills: None.

YOUNG & INEXPERIENCED CYCLISTS

The route to Selby is mainly traffic-free and flat, with short sections on quiet lanes in Riccall and Barlby.

On the route to Beningbrough, the last 5 miles (8km) follow quiet country lanes.

Cycle facilities throughout York are excellent and children could easily manage a ride in either direction from there.

REFRESHMENTS

- Lots of choice in Selby and York, including the famous Betty's Café Tea Rooms in St Helen's Square. There is also plenty of choice in Riccall and Bishopthorpe.
- The Sidings Hotel & Restaurant, Shipton (open for coffee, lunch, tea).
- The cafe at Beningbrough Hall is open from Easter to October.
- Downay Arms pub, Blacksmith Arms pub, Newton-on-Ouse (just beyond Beningbrough).

THINGS TO SEE & DO

- **York Minster:** 0844 939 0011; www.yorkminster.org
- **National Railway Museum:** 08448 153139; www.nrm.org.uk
- **York Castle Museum:** 01904 687687; www.yorkcastlemuseum.org.uk
- **Jorvik Viking Centre:** 01904 615505; www.jorvik-viking-centre.co.uk
- **Clifford's Tower:** William the Conqueror built the castle for his northern campaign of terror in 1069. At various points in its history, Clifford's Tower became a royal mint, functioned as a prison, gruesomely displayed the bodies of leaders of uprisings, and was even a court; www.english-heritage.org.uk
- **Treasurer's House:** a fine 17th- and 18th-century house near the historic York Minster; 01904 624247; www.nationaltrust.org.uk
- **Fairfax House:** one of England's finest Georgian townhouses; 01904 655 543; www.fairfaxhouse.co.uk
- **Merchant Adventurers' Hall:** medieval guildhall dating from 1357; 01904 654818; www.theyorkcompany.co.uk
- **Selby Abbey:** 01757 705123; www.selbyabbey.org.uk
- **Beningbrough Hall & Gardens:** 01904 472027; www.nationaltrust.org.uk

Clifford's Tower in York

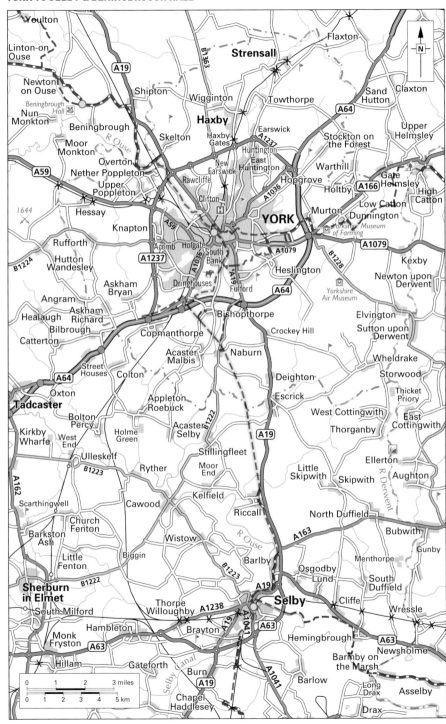

York to Selby cycle track

TRAIN STATIONS
Selby; York.

BIKE HIRE
- Bob Trotter Cycles: 01904 622868; www.bobtrottercycles.com
- Cycle Heaven, York station: 01904 651870; www.cycle-heaven.co.uk
- York Cycle Hire: 01904 632226; www.yorkcyclehire.com

FURTHER INFORMATION
- To view or print National Cycle Network routes, visit www.sustrans.org.uk
- Maps for this area are available to buy from www.sustransshop.co.uk
- York Tourist Information: 01904 550099; www.visityork.org

ROUTE DESCRIPTION
Travelling south, leave York station via the ramp from the end of the short-stay car park towards the River Ouse to join the riverside path. The route follows the riverside path southwards through the city, under Skeldergate Bridge and alongside Rowntree Park. This part of the route is also signed as the Trans Pennine Trail and takes you past Knavesmire Wood and through York's famous racecourse.

Adjacent to the A64 turn left onto the York to Selby Path and follow the popular railway path all the way to Riccall. Turn right into York Road and follow the NCN65 signs along Main Street to rejoin the former railway path. In Barlby follow the NCN65 signs into York Road, past Barlby Hall and into Barlby Road and then Barlby Crescent before rejoining the path along the river into the market town of Selby.

To travel northwards towards Beningbrough from York station, again leave the station following the new cycling ramps, and following the signs for NCN65 to the River Ouse. Cross the Ouse and head left on the east bank of the river. Follow the course of the river, crossing the grazed Rawcliffe Meadows, to Skelton. There you turn left onto Overton Road to Shipton, where you follow the signs left onto Shipton Low Road and on to reach Beningbrough Hall.

NEARBY CYCLE ROUTES
York is at a crossroads of the NCN. The north–south section from Middlesbrough to Selby and Doncaster is signed and mapped (National Route 65), as is the route from Beverley and Pocklington to the east (National Route 66). The western section to Harrogate and Leeds is still to be completed. For other nearby routes, cross the Millennium Bridge for a route through Walmgate Stray, past the University to the Foss Island Railway Path and on to Stamford Bridge, signed as National Route 66. Also, there are plenty of local cycling links through York.

RIVER HUMBER – HESSLE TO HOWDEN

The Humber is a mighty river that drains one-fifth of the area of England. It's the river and its estuary that are the principal features of this ride, together with the modern Humber Bridge, now the fifth-largest single-span suspension bridge in the world, and historic Howden Minster. Starting at the foot of one of the massive towers that support the Humber Bridge, you follow the river inland to where the Humber begins at the confluence of the Trent and the Ouse, before following the Ouse through to Howden. Take time to admire the engineering achievement of the Humber Bridge. Opened in 1981, it spans over a mile (1.6km) and is constantly moving. In winds of 80mph (129km/h), it bends in the middle by more than 3m (10ft). Proof that the Humber was also an important waterway 4,000 years ago came with the discoveries of three Bronze Age boats at North Ferriby between 1937 and 1963.

Further along the ride, the RSPB's reserve at Blacktoft Sands is home to a great range of wetland and reed-bed birds. Stop occasionally and scale the bank of the flood embankment to take in the open views over the estuary, mudflats and salt marshes.

The small market town of Howden stands out a mile, thanks to the tower of the 13th-century Minster by the Market Place, set among the town's well-preserved Georgian architecture. Until the 1920s, its famous horse fair drew buyers from all over Europe and up to 16,000 horses would change hands during the week.

ROUTE INFORMATION

National Route: 65
Start: Humber Bridge Viewpoint, Cliff Road, Hessle.
Finish: Howden Market Place.

Distance: 24 miles (38.5km). Shorter option: from Humber Bridge to Blacktoft 17 miles (27.5km).
Grade: Medium.
Surface: Tarmac road and path, plus two gravel

Humber Bridge

Black-headed gull collecting nest material

track sections.
Hills: One hill between Welton and Elloughton.

YOUNG & INEXPERIENCED CYCLISTS

Although much of this route is on-road, don't let that put you off. These are very quiet lanes, with only a few places where you will encounter moderate traffic.

REFRESHMENTS

- Lots of choice in Hessle, including the Country Park Inn.
- Pubs in North Ferriby, Welton, Elloughton, Brantingham, Ellerker, Blacktoft and Laxton.
- Lots of choice in Howden.

THINGS TO SEE & DO

- Humber Bridge: admire the engineering that made this the longest suspension bridge in the world for many years; there's a high viewpoint in nearby Humber Bridge Country Park, Hessle; www.humberbridge.co.uk
- RSPB Blacktoft Sands nature reserve: largest tidal reed bed in England, with 270 species of birds; 01405 704665;

www.rspb.org.uk/blacktoftsands
- Howden Minster: partially ruined cathedral-like church, with parts dating from the 13th century; 01430 432056; www.english-heritage.org.uk

TRAIN STATIONS

The following stations are close to the route: Ferriby, Brough, Broomfleet and Saltmarshe.

BIKE HIRE

None locally.

FURTHER INFORMATION

- To view or print National Cycle Network routes, visit www.sustrans.org.uk
- Maps for this area are available to buy from www.sustransshop.co.uk
- Trans Pennine Trail: www.transpenninetrail.org.uk
- Humber Bridge Tourist Information: 01482 647161; www.humberbridge.co.uk
- Hull and East Yorkshire Tourist Information: 01482 223559; www.hullandeastyorkshire.com

ROUTE DESCRIPTION

Follow the road under the Humber Bridge and through the hotel grounds onto a path along the foreshore towards North Ferriby. This path affords one of the best views of the bridge, so remember to look back once in a while. Before you leave the riverside in North Ferriby, explore the parkland area by the flagpoles to find out about the Bronze Age boat excavations.

Follow the road under the railway and turn left at the crossroads to join an off-road path alongside the A63. Use the bridge to cross this busy dual carriageway and continue parallel to the road. Turn right up the side of the school

Ruins of Howden Minster

and left onto the road in Welton. Fork right into Parliament Street and go straight on into Kidd Lane for the only real climb on the ride as you skirt the edge of the Yorkshire Wolds. Have a rest at the top and find a gap in the hedge to take in the view.

Follow signs for the Trans Pennine Trail through Elloughton and Brantingham to reach Ellerker. As you leave the village, turn left for Broomfleet. At the end of Broomfleet, the route turns left onto a gravel track to Weighton Lock and carries on to Blacktoft. Climb the flood bank to see if there are any ships moored at the jetty – larger vessels lay up here and wait for the tide to rise before making their way upstream to Goole.

The route winds along quiet lanes but after Yokefleet there are a couple of turns to look out for. First, make sure you turn left into Metham Lane towards Laxton. Then, after passing through Laxton, make sure you turn right for Kilpin at a crossroads. Once in Kilpin, turn left for Howden.

Soon you come to the motorway, which you cross over. Howden will then be in sight. Go straight over at the roundabout, then right for the centre of Howden and left into the Market Place.

NEARBY CYCLE ROUTES

This ride is on the eastern part of the Trans Pennine Trail (National Routes 65 and 62), which runs between Southport and Hornsea, and Leeds and Chesterfield (Route 67).

National Route 1 goes south over the Humber Bridge, which has cycle lanes on both sides. Northwards, it goes from Hull to Beverley, an attractive minster town on the edge of the Wolds.

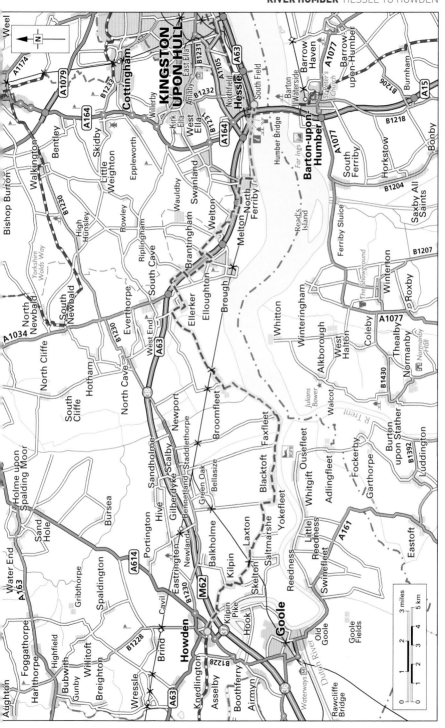

HORNSEA RAIL TRAIL – HULL TO HORNSEA

This ride will take you from the Humber estuary, out of the ancient seafaring city and across the rich agricultural landscape of the Holderness Plain to finish on the seafront at the resort of Hornsea, the eastern end of the Trans Pennine Trail. Hornsea Mere is Yorkshire's largest freshwater lake, but less than a mile (1.6km) from the sea. For virtually the whole length you follow the track bed of the old Hull to Hornsea Railway that used to carry people to the coast. Make sure you allow some time to visit Hull's award-winning attraction, The Deep, one of the most spectacular aquariums in the world and home to 40 sharks and over 3,500 fish. Have a stroll around the Old Town and docks area, and visit at least one of Hull's many free museums. The name Kingston-upon-Hull comes from the first Charter to the port on the River Hull given by King Edward I in 1299 (King's Town). Today, Hull has around 80 miles (129km) of cycle routes, on- and off-road, and has the fifth highest cycle-to-work use in the UK.

ROUTE INFORMATION
National Route: 65
Start: The Deep submarium, Hull.
Finish: The Sea Mark, Hornsea seafront.
Distance: 15 miles (24km).
Grade: Easy.
Surface: Tarmac road and paths, and gravel tracks.
Hills: None.

YOUNG & INEXPERIENCED CYCLISTS
The first part of the ride is on busy roads with cycle lanes, and there are several minor roads to cross, including the A165 just before the

halfway point. A roundabout in Hornsea can also be busy when there are lots of people heading to the beach.

REFRESHMENTS
- Lots of choice in Hull and Hornsea, including the cafe at Hornsea Mere.
- Pubs in New Ellerby and Great Hatfield, just off the route.

THINGS TO SEE & DO
Hull:
- **The Deep:** the world's only submarium, telling the story of the oceans; 01482 381000; www.thedeep.co.uk
- **Museums Quarter, High Street:** links Streetlife Museum, Hull & East Riding Museum and Wilberforce House; 01482 300300; www.hullcc.gov.uk/museumcollections
- **Arctic Corsair, High Street:** a deep-sea trawler converted into a museum, with free guided tours; 01482 300300; www.hullcc.gov.uk
- **Maritime Museum, Queen Victoria Square:** artefacts from Hull's early 19th-century whaling fleet; 01482 300300; www.hullcc.gov.uk
- **Spurn Lightship, Hull Marina:** former navigation aid in the treacherous River

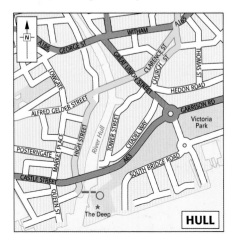

HULL

The Deep submarium, Hull

Humber, now a 'crewed' museum; 01482 300300; www.hullcc.gov.uk

Hornsea:
- **Hornsea Museum:** village life through the ages in an 18th-century farmhouse; 01964 533443; www.hornseamuseum.com
- **Hornsea Mere:** large freshwater lake with bird reserve and boats for hire; 01964 533433

TRAIN STATIONS
Hull Paragon Interchange.

BIKE HIRE
None locally.

FURTHER INFORMATION
- To view or print National Cycle Network

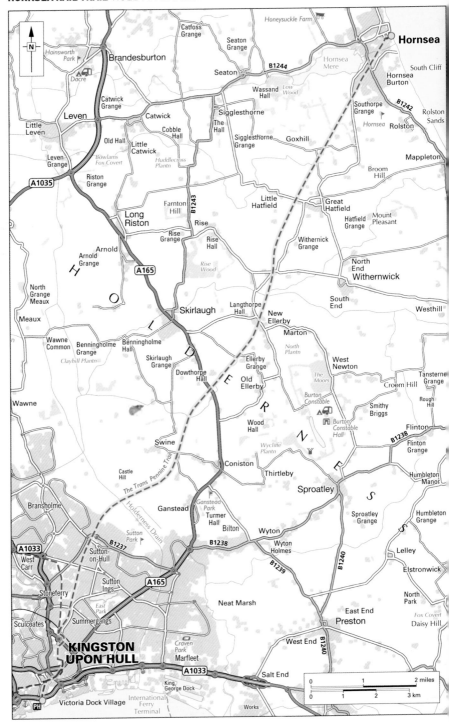

Hornsea promenade

routes, visit www.sustrans.org.uk
- Maps for this area are available to buy from www.sustransshop.co.uk
- Trans Pennine Trail: www.transpenninetrail.org.uk
- Hull and East Yorkshire Tourist Information: 01482 223559; www.visithullandeastyorkshire.com

ROUTE DESCRIPTION

From The Deep, cross the new bridge over the River Hull and turn right to follow the signed cycle route towards the city centre and the Trans Pennine Trail. Turn left into George Yard and then right to join the main Trans Pennine Trail (National Route 65) on Alfred Gelder Street and over Drypool Bridge. At the traffic lights, go straight on into Dansom Lane. After a few hundred metres, turn right onto the off-road path that takes you almost to Hornsea.

An underpass takes you under a busy road, before a road crossing. Be sure to follow the Trans Pennine Trail and Hornsea signs, as there are several cycle routes in this area – you need to turn off right just after passing under a railway bridge. From here, route finding is easy; just take care at the road crossings.

A bridge over the trail and the start of a tarmac path mark the run-in towards Hornsea.

At the end of the path, go through the gate and left to follow Marlborough Road. At the roundabout, your route is on the ramp straight ahead, best accessed along Bank Terrace (third exit on the roundabout). Once on the ramp, carry on until you reach the red-brick former station, where the landscaped Hornsea Gateway formally welcomes you to town. Straight ahead, you'll see the seafront and the bronze Sea Mark that marks the easternmost point on the Trans Pennine Trail.

NEARBY CYCLE ROUTES

This ride is on the eastern part of the Trans Pennine Trail (National Routes 65 and 62), which runs between Southport and Hornsea, and Leeds and Chesterfield (Route 67).

The South Holderness Rail Trail spurs off Route 65 east of Hull and goes through the attractive small market town of Hedon as far as Ottringham. Just west of the city is the high-spanning Humber Bridge, which has cycle lanes on both sides and is worth a visit on a clear day, following Routes 1 and 65. The historic town of Beverley on the edge of the Wolds lies just to the north of Hull on National Routes 1 and 66.

FYLDE COAST – BLACKPOOL TO FLEETWOOD

This is a magnificent coastal ride running the whole length of the Blackpool, Cleveleys and Fleetwood Promenades. You are never far from the sea and the beaches, which you can join at numerous points. On the Tuesday prior to the switch-on of Blackpool Illuminations each year, you can 'Ride the Lights'. This is when Blackpool closes 6 miles (9.5km) of the main coastal road from Squires Gate in the south to Red Bank, to allow thousands of cyclists a first sight of the town's famous illuminations, which have been a major part of Blackpool's attraction since 1879, when they were described as 'artificial sunshine'. This is a memorable family occasion, which has introduced cycling to many.

Although this ride starts at North Pier, impressive coastal defence works, finished off in sweeping curves of sand-coloured concrete, lead south for another 3 miles (5km), past the awesome rides of the Pleasure Beach and the sculptures alluding to the romance of a Blackpool holiday. Note that engineering works to strengthen the coastline are almost always ongoing. Where diversions entail running alongside the tramway, itself an attraction with a wide range of antique vehicles on the tracks (do be careful not to slip into the tracks!), the smooth concrete either side of the rails is a tempting route.

ROUTE INFORMATION
National Route: 62
Start: North Pier, Blackpool.
Finish: Lower Lighthouse, Fleetwood.
Distance: 9 miles (14.5km).
Grade: Easy.

Surface: Tarmac or concrete promenades.
Hills: None.

YOUNG & INEXPERIENCED CYCLISTS
This ride is ideal for young and novice cyclists – an almost perfect seafront experience.

Blackpool Pier and ferris wheel

'Glam Rocks' by
Peter Freeman

REFRESHMENTS

- Lots of choice in Blackpool and Fleetwood.
- Taste Cafe Bar, north end of Cleveleys Promenade.
- North Euston Hotel, Fleetwood.
- Cafe at Marine Hall, Fleetwood.

THINGS TO SEE & DO
Blackpool:

- **Blackpool Tower:** a 158m (518ft) structure based on the Eiffel Tower; variety of attractions; 01253 622242; www.theblackpooltower.com
- **Blackpool Solaris Centre:** one of the first of Blackpool's council buildings to integrate a high level of energy-efficient features in its design; set in 4 acres of garden land; environmental exhibitions; 01253 478020; www.solariscentre.org
- **Blackpool Pleasure Beach:** huge funfair park; 0871 222 1234; www.blackpoolpleasurebeach.com
- **North, Central and South Piers:** all within walking distance along the Golden Mile, which also includes Louis Tussaud's Waxworks and the Sea Life Centre.

Fleetwood:

- **Fleetwood Museum:** explores the story of Fleetwood from past to present; set in the old Custom House designed by the 19th-century architect Decimus Burton; overlooks beautiful Morecambe Bay; 01253 876621; www.lancashire.gov.uk/education/museums
- **Fleetwood Market:** large traditional market, over 100 years old; www.fleetwoodmarket.co.uk

TRAIN STATIONS
Blackpool North; Blackpool South.

BIKE HIRE

- **Hire-a-Bike, Cycle Blackpool:** pay-as-you-cycle network; 01253 320094; www.hourbike.com/blackpool
- **Waterfront Wheels, Marine Hall, Fleetwood:**

RIDE 15

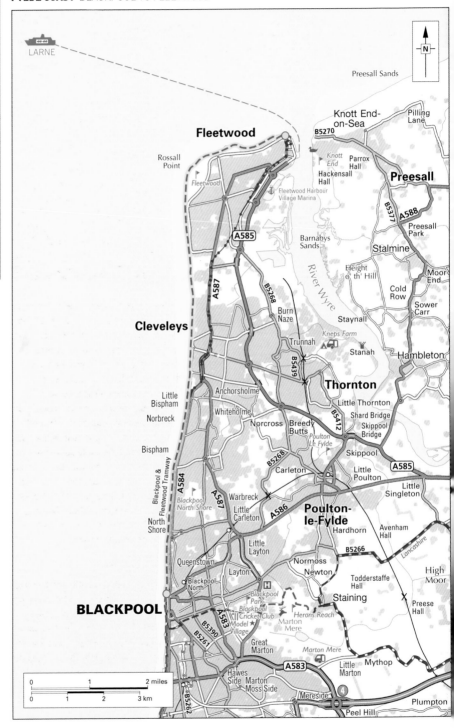

Blackpool Tower and sandy beach

adapted bicycles for people with low mobility or disabilities; 01253 771141

FURTHER INFORMATION

- To view or print National Cycle Network routes visit www.sustrans.org.uk
- Maps for this area are available to buy from www.sustransshop.co.uk
- Blackpool Tourist Information: 01253 478222; www.visitblackpool.com
- Thornton Cleveleys Tourist Information: 01253 853378; www.wyrebc.gov.uk
- Fleetwood Tourist Information: 01253 773953
- Wyre Tourist Information: www.visitwyre.co.uk

ROUTE DESCRIPTION

North Pier is a little north of Blackpool Tower – you can't miss it! And the route is clearly signed. Note that in this part of Blackpool there are often a number of different levels of promenade – those close to the sea, and those higher up near the tram route, with wider views. The cycle route generally follows the higher levels, and it is here, along the Queen's Promenade, that the main lighting tableaux are located. Once past Red Bank Tram Stop (unfortunately, you can't take bikes on trams), the path follows a wide stretch of grassland

down to Little Bispham, where the tram veers away from the sea on its journey to Fleetwood.

One of the advantages of a promenade route in a seaside resort is that you are never far from refreshments, fish and chips, public gardens and the beach itself. There is no reason at all for pressing on immediately through Cleveleys, which is a good stopping-off point before the slightly emptier run around Rossall Point. Here, the promenade is bounded by the golf course, and the route seems more windblown and sandier than it was to the south.

Finally, you curve away from the sea to end at Fleetwood Lower Lighthouse, which marks the navigation channel to the River Wyre and the entrance to the docks, as well as the terminus for the Blackpool trams.

NEARBY CYCLE ROUTES

At Fleetwood, a ferry takes people and bikes to Knott End-on-Sea and the country lanes of Over Wyre. Note that its schedules are affected by weather and tides. From North Pier, National Route 62 cuts inland to the magnificent Stanley Park, Blackpool Zoo and model village and into the rural Wyre countryside towards Preston. South from Squires Gate, you can cycle via the Lytham St Annes Promenade to reach Preston on a seaside route.

LUNE VALLEY

Throughout the 18th century, Lancaster was England's principal port for trade with America. Myriad Georgian houses around the centre of the town date back to this era of prosperity. Going further back in time, the keep of Lancaster Castle is Norman, standing 24m (79ft) high with walls 3m (10ft) thick. The castle also served as the county jail; among the many notable prisoners was the Quaker leader George Fox, who was imprisoned in the 17th century. There are superb views of the surrounding countryside from the Ashton Memorial, built in 1909.

Reflecting the city's maritime heritage, the Millennium Bridge is the centrepiece of the city's cycle network and stands on the location of the first bridge over the River Lune. One route leads to Morecambe and its curving 4-mile (6.5km) promenade, with views across Morecambe Bay to the mountains of the Lake District. A second option follows the lovely, majestic River Lune north to the Crook O'Lune, with views north to the hills of the Yorkshire Dales. Lastly, to the south, you can cycle to Glasson Dock along the railway path. The canal link to Glasson was built in 1826 in response to the demands from Lancaster merchants for a larger port, so that they could increase their imports of sugar, cotton and other commodities from Africa, America and the West Indies.

ROUTE INFORMATION

National Routes: 6, 69
Start: Millennium Bridge, Lancaster.
Finish: Morecambe train station, or Crook O'Lune picnic site, or Glasson Dock.
Distance: Lancaster to Morecambe train station 3 miles (5km); Lancaster to Crook O'Lune 4 miles (6.5km); Lancaster to Glasson Dock 5 miles (8km).
Grade: Easy.
Surface: Tarmac or fine gravel path.
Hills: None.

YOUNG & INEXPERIENCED CYCLISTS

Ideal for novices and children; mostly traffic-free with no busy road crossings.

Signpost on National Route 69

Crossing the Lune Bridge

Bronze statue of Eric Morecambe

REFRESHMENTS
- Lots of choice in Lancaster and Morecambe.
- Pubs just off the route in Halton and Caton.
- Pubs and other choices in Glasson.

THINGS TO SEE & DO
Lancaster:
- **Lancaster Castle:** Grade I listed building, with parts dating back to the 12th century; 01524 64998; www.lancastercastle.com
- **City Museum:** covers Lancaster's history from Roman times to the present day; 01524 64637; www.lancashire.gov.uk

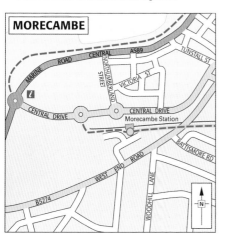

- **Tropical Butterfly House:** situated on the east side of town in Williamson Park; 01524 33318; www.citycoastcountryside.co.uk
- **Maritime Museum:** award-winning museum housed in the former Port of Lancaster Custom House; 01524 382264; www.lancashire.gov.uk

Morecambe:
- **Morecambe Promenade:** a vast collection of public artworks forms part of the promenade and sea defences; www.visitnorthwest.com
- **Winter Gardens:** Grade II listed; built in 1897; www.thewintergardensmorecambe.co.uk
- **Eric Morecambe statue:** tribute in bronze to Morecambe's most famous son.

TRAIN STATIONS
Lancaster; Morecambe.

BIKE HIRE
- **Cycle Adventure, Lancaster:** 07518 373007; www.cycle-adventure.co.uk
- **Leisure Lakes Bikes, Lancaster:** 01524 844389; www.leisurelakesbikes.co.uk
- **Sunshine Cycles Morecambe:** 01524 414709; www.sunshinecyclehire.co.uk

FURTHER INFORMATION
- To view or print National Cycle Network

LUNE VALLEY

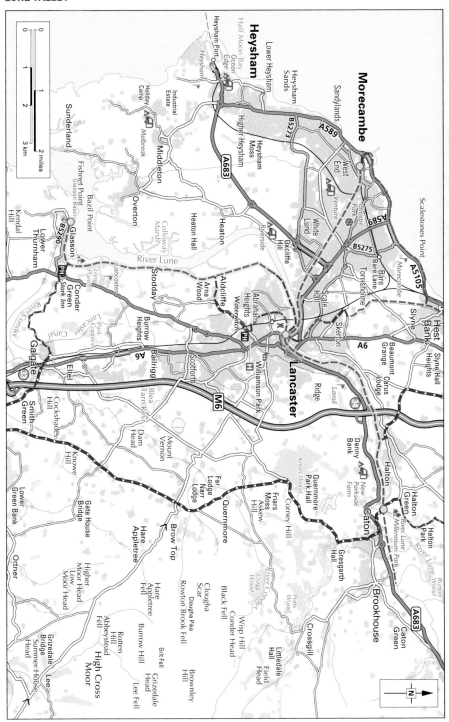

Cycling along
Morecambe prom

routes, visit www.sustrans.org.uk
- Maps for this area are available to buy from www.sustransshop.co.uk
- **Morecambe Tourist Information:** 01524 582808; www.citycoastcountryside.co.uk
- **Lancaster Tourist Information:** 01524 582394; www.citycoastcountryside.co.uk

ROUTE DESCRIPTION

For the route to Morecambe, cross the Millennium Bridge, and take the path on the north side of the River Lune. This leads to the railway path, which takes you through a largely urban area all the way to the train station in Morecambe. From here, it is just a short ride on quiet streets to the seafront.

To cycle to the Crook O'Lune picnic site, keep on the south side of the Millennium Bridge and follow the traffic-free path east alongside the River Lune. You'll travel through mixed woodland before going under the mighty stone aqueduct carrying the canal, then beneath the M6 motorway bridge, and twice crossing the river at the Crook O'Lune, where the river describes a U-shaped bend between Halton and Caton. Along the way are interpretation boards with details of some of the birds you may see along the river.

To ride to Glasson Dock, start at the southern end of the Millennium Bridge and ride on roads through the St George's Quay area, following signs to Glasson. When the road ends, continue on a narrower, surfaced track through open countryside to join the disused railway line alongside the Lune Estuary and salt marshes. Continue by Conder Green – a good picnic site – beside the sea wall to reach Glasson Dock.

NEARBY CYCLE ROUTES

National Route 6 passes through Lancaster on its way from Preston to Kendal. National Route 62 will eventually run close to the coast southwest of Glasson Dock to Fleetwood and Blackpool. National Route 72 explores South Lakeland on its way to Barrow. Further east, the Pennine Cycleway links Settle to Appleby-in-Westmorland.

Other waymarked or traffic-free rides include:
- The towpath of the Lancaster Canal, which can be followed through Lancaster and north to Carnforth (National Route 6).
- The Lancashire Cycleway, which uses Regional Routes 90 and 91 to link Carnforth, Lancaster and Blackpool, and circle the Forest of Bowland on a splendid 260-mile (418km) ride.

KENDAL TO GRANGE-OVER-SANDS

Kendal is the main town of Cumbria's South Lakeland district and known as a gateway to the Lake District National Park. This ride, however, is across much more gently undulating Morecambe Bay limestone country to the sedate Edwardian seaside resort of Grange-over-Sands, separated from a marshy part of the bay by a mile (1.6km) long promenade.

It's always an idea to stock up on some of Kendal's famous energy-giving mintcake before heading away from the centre's maze of 'yards' and 'ginnels' along the now filled-in Lancaster Canal. Following and eventually crossing the River Kent leads you to Sizergh Fell, where Sizergh Castle sits amid acres of parkland. The castle was constructed around the original 13th-century pele tower, to afford protection during the border raids of the Middle Ages. Across the wide, flat floor of the Lyth Valley, famous for its damson orchards, limestone escarpments rise up from low-lying pastures and mosslands by the Kent Estuary. There are lovely views across to the Arnside & Silverdale Area of Outstanding Natural Beauty (AONB) and of South Lakeland fells in the other direction.

ROUTE INFORMATION
National Route: 6
Regional Route: 20
Start: Canal head below the west side of Kendal Castle.
Finish: Grange-over-Sands train station.
Distance: 15 miles (24km). Shorter option: from the canal head to Sizergh Castle 5.5 miles (9km).
Grade: Easy to medium.
Surface: Mostly good tarmac on roads and canal path. Short section of the old canal path can be muddy in places after wet weather.
Hills: None (by Lake District standards), but there's one short steep climb after Sizergh, with a similarly steep descent through Levens village to the floor of the Lyth Valley. Care should be taken at corners on the descent. Otherwise, the ride is flat or rolling terrain.

YOUNG & INEXPERIENCED CYCLISTS
The first part of the ride is on a flat, shared-use, traffic-free path, with a couple of road crossings to be negotiated. After this, it's usually quiet roads to Grange-over-Sands and care should be taken on narrower sections, especially in summer when hedges can restrict visibility. Approaching Grange, the route joins the busier B5277. It is possible to dismount and push your bike along the pavement into the town and onto the long promenade (where cycling is not officially permitted).

REFRESHMENTS
- Lots of choice in Kendal.
- Tearoom at Low Sizergh Barn.
- Licensed cafe at Sizergh Castle.
- Strickland Arms pub, close to Sizergh Castle.
- Hare and Hounds pub, Levens.
- Gilpin Bridge Inn, Gilpin Bridge.
- The Derby Arms, Witherslack.
- Lots of choice in Grange-over-Sands.

THINGS TO SEE & DO
Kendal:
- Kendal Castle: medieval ruins, with a good view over the town.
- Museum of Lakeland Life, Abbott Hall, opposite side of the River Kent to Kendal Castle: explores the rich social history and traditional heritage of Cumbria; 01539 722464; www.lakelandmuseum.org.uk

Sizergh:
- Low Sizergh Barn: organic farm with trail, shop and craft gallery; 01539 560426; www.lowsizerghbarn.co.uk
- Sizergh Castle & Garden: grand medieval manor house surrounded by beautiful

Kendal seen from Castle Hill

gardens; 01539 560951;
www.nationaltrust.org.uk

TRAIN STATIONS
Kendal; Oxenholme; Grange-over-Sands.

BIKE HIRE
- Wheelbase, Staveley: 01539 821443;
  www.wheelbase.co.uk

FURTHER INFORMATION
- To view or print National Cycle Network
  routes, visit www.sustrans.org.uk
- Maps for this area are available to buy from
  www.sustransshop.co.uk
- Kendal Tourist Information: 01539 735891
- Grange-over-Sands Tourist Information:
  01539 534026; www.golakes.co.uk

Canalside cycling at Kendal on Route 6

ROUTE DESCRIPTION
Starting at the old canal head by the ski slope
and below Kendal Castle, pick up the tarmac
cyclepath along the route of the old canal (now
filled in). Go along this for a couple of miles,
crossing two roads, to Natland Road, following
blue signs for National Route 6 towards

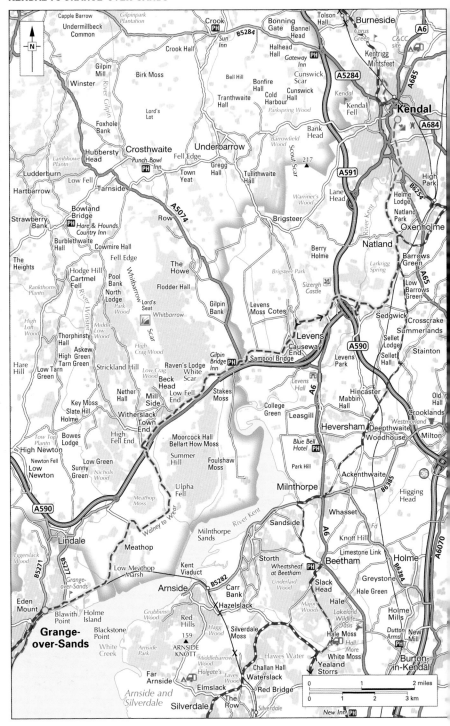

Morecambe Bay seen from Grange-over-Sands

Lancaster. Shortly after passing Natland, Route 6 turns left uphill but, instead, you continue straight on to Sedgwick, go under the old stone canal bridge and keep following the blue signs for Regional Route 20 (Walney to Wear & Whitby – W2W) across the River Kent and all the way to Grange.

The cycle track and wooden bridge just past the Gilpin Bridge Inn avoid having to cross the busy A590, and the parallel minor road takes you all the way to Witherslack. At the crossroads by the Derby Arms, turn left. Then bear right just before the road joins the dual carriageway, to go through a tunnel underneath – watch out for other users coming out. Follow the road through Meathop, around the mound of Meathop Fell and across the River Winster.

At the junction with the busier B road into Grange-over-Sands, turn left. Look out on your left for the path to a footbridge over the railway, leading you onto the promenade and to the train station, pushing your bike (cycling is not yet permitted on the promenade).

Otherwise, stay on the road to the station's main entrance. You can get onto the promenade from here as well.

NEARBY CYCLE ROUTES
National Route 6 continues north of Kendal to Staveley and Windermere. Going south, you can follow it to Carnforth and Lancaster. Kendal is on the Walney to Wear & Whitby (W2W) coast-to-coast cycle route (www.cyclingw2w.info).

ROWRAH TO WHITEHAVEN & WORKINGTON

The west coast of Cumbria is criss-crossed with old mineral railways, many of which have been converted to cycling and walking routes. The C2C, the most famous of all the long-distance cycle routes on the National Cycle Network, has two starting points here: Workington and Whitehaven. This ride runs from Rowrah on the edge of the Lake District National Park at Cleator Moor, northeast to Whitehaven, and then along the coast to Workington, finishing at the new Navvies Bridge, rebuilt in 2011 after its predecessor was washed away in the terrible floods of 2009.

Whitehaven, once a small fishing village, developed as a port in the 17th century with the discovery of coal and very high grade iron ore. Its Georgian and Victorian buildings reflect the prosperity of this era. Workington is an ancient market town at the mouth of the River Derwent that became a major industrial town and port in the 18th century, with the exploitation of the local iron ore and coal pits. The ride between Rowrah and Workington can be completed as one or in two halves, using Whitehaven as a start point.

Whitehaven harbour and church

ROUTE INFORMATION

National Routes: 71, 72
Start and Finish: Rowrah Hall Farm; Whitehaven harbour front; Navvies Bridge, Workington.
Distance: Rowrah to Whitehaven 9 miles (14km); Whitehaven to Workington 7 miles (11km).
Grade: Fairly easy. Predominantly traffic-free route with some short on-road sections around Whitehaven and in central Workington.
Surface: Tarmac and compacted stone dust.
Hills: Some uphill gradients but nothing too severe.

YOUNG & INEXPERIENCED CYCLISTS

The traffic-free sections are suitable for riders of all ages and experience. On-road sections follow predominantly quiet roads.

REFRESHMENTS

- You're spoilt for choice in both Workington and Whitehaven.

THINGS TO SEE & DO

- **The Rum Story:** the word's first exhibition depicting the story of the UK rum trade; 01946 592933; www.rumstory.co.uk
- **The Beacon:** situated on the attractive harbourside in Whitehaven and home to the town's museum collection. It traces the social, industrial and maritime heritage of the area, using local characters, audio-visual displays and fascinating museum pieces. There is a Met Office weather centre exhibition on the top floor offering panoramic views of the town, the coast, and across the Solway Firth to Scotland; 01946 598914; www.thebeacon-whitehaven.co.uk
- **Harrington Reservoir Nature Reserve:** 01946 831535; www.harrington-nature-reserve.org.uk

TRAIN STATIONS

Whitehaven; Corkickle; Parton; Harrington; Workington.

BIKE HIRE

- Haven Cycles, Whitehaven: 01946 63263; www.havencycles-c2cservices.co.uk
- Ainfield Cycle Centre, Cleator: 01946 812427
- Braemar Bikes, Whitehaven: 01946 693009
- Southside Cycles, Whitehaven: 01946 591004
- Bike Bank, Workington: 01900 603 337.

FURTHER INFORMATION

- To view or print National Cycle Network routes, visit www.sustrans.org.uk
- Maps for this area are available to buy from www.sustransshop.co.uk

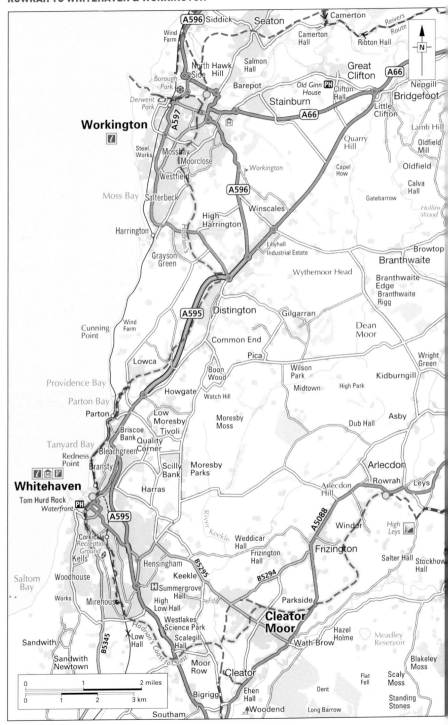

- **Cumbria Tourist Information:** 01946 852939; www.visitcumbria.com

ROUTE DESCRIPTION

Starting at Rowrah Hall Farm, the route heads east on a traffic-free path following signs for NCN71. The route continues southwest through the village of Parkside and to the north of Cleator Moor. As you cross Blind Lane, bear to the left and as you reach the village of Moor Row take the right turn, following the signs for NCN72 to Whitehaven. The route continues east and then turns north through Mirehouse. After a short section on quiet residential roads, the route rejoins the traffic-free path following Pow Beck stream through Corkickle. A short on-road section as you reach the centre of Whitehaven takes you straight to the harbour where you enjoy a traffic-free ride along the harbour-front. Another short section on-road near North Pier takes you to North Beach, where you join the traffic-free path along the coast at Redness Point, with beautiful views out to sea. Another short on-road section at Parton takes you past Parton railway station and the Roman fort. Follow the NCN72 signs and turn right at Stamford Hill Avenue to join the traffic-free path at Lowca. The route crosses over the A595, travels through Distington, and then re-crosses the A595 and heads past High Harrington. Stay on the traffic-free path through the outskirts of Workington before a final short on-road

section. This takes you straight across Oxford Street in the town centre and on to the walking and cycling path across Navvies Bridge.

NEARBY CYCLE ROUTES

- Heading east from Rowrah, beyond Kirkland you can continue northeast on a mixture of quiet lanes and wide stone tracks to explore the stunning scenery alongside Ennerdale Water.
- There are also waymarked woodland routes in Whinlatter Forest and the Keswick Railway Path to Threlkeld.
- At Cleator Moor you can follow NCN72 south along the coast to Seascale.
- Heading north from Workington across Navvies Bridge you are on the famous C2C long-distance cycle route which goes all the way to Tynemouth.

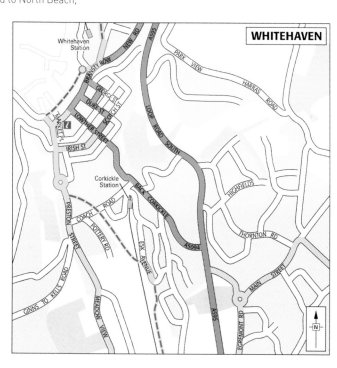

SOLWAY COAST FROM BURGH BY SANDS

The Solway Coast Area of Outstanding Natural Beauty (AONB) stretches from Rockcliffe Marsh on the Scottish Border to just north of the historic harbour town of Maryport. It also has parts of Hadrian's Wall World Heritage Site, with Bowness-on-Solway being the western end of Hadrian's Wall Path National Trail. For this ride, you'll be on Hadrian's Cycleway (National Route 72), which extends round the Cumbrian coastline to Ravenglass.

Saltmarsh, farmland, wet grasslands and raised mires (peat bogs) are what make this area so special. They are all home to a great variety of wildlife, wading birds in particular. Fine views across the Solway Firth to Scotland's Dumfries & Galloway coastline, the prominent hill of Criffel and the Northern Lakeland fells form part of the unique backdrop to this ride.

Look out for the statue of Edward I by the entrance to the pub in Burgh by Sands, a reminder of when England and Scotland were waging war. The village church is constructed from stone from Hadrian's Wall and the Roman fort upon which it is built.

You might see some 'haaf netting' in the Solway, a unique method of fishing that's been practised since Viking times. When you next check your watch or clock, remember that the time signal is now transmitted from Anthorn radio station, just outside Anthorn village.

ROUTE INFORMATION
National Route: 72
Start: Burgh by Sands.
Finish: Burgh by Sands.
Distance: 24 miles (38.5km). Shorter option: from Burgh by Sands to Bowness-on-Solway

16 miles (25.5km).
Grade: Easy, although a prevailing westerly headwind will make it harder initially.
Surface: Tarmac.
Hills: None.

Panoramic view across Solway Firth

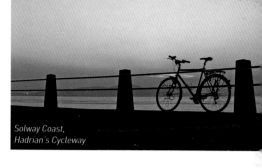

*Solway Coast,
Hadrian's Cycleway*

YOUNG & INEXPERIENCED CYCLISTS

These are quiet roads on very gently undulating terrain, with just a couple of very short steeper bits where the road rises up away from the shoreline.

REFRESHMENTS

- The Greyhound pub, Burgh by Sands.
- Laal Bite self-service tuck shop, Drumburgh.
- Highland Laddie Inn, Glasson.
- Hope & Anchor pub, Port Carlisle.
- Kings Arms pub, Bowness-on-Solway.

THINGS TO SEE & DO

- **King Edward I Monument, Burgh by Sands:** erected where Edward I, 'Hammer of the Scots', is believed to have died on 7 July 1307 while preparing to cross the Solway and do battle with Robert the Bruce.
- **St Michael's Church, Burgh by Sands:** Norman church with a fortified tower to protect against raiders from across the border.
- **Glasson Moss:** some of the best pristine lowland raised bog in the country; www.naturalengland.org.uk

- **RSPB Campfield Marsh nature reserve, aproaching Bowness-on-Solway:** a range of habitats and native wildlife; cycle racks; 01697 351330; www.rspb.org.uk
- **The Banks, Bowness-on-Solway:** Roman-style wooden shelter with interpretative panels overlooking the Solway; official western end of Hadrian's Wall Path National Trail, off the main village road.

TRAIN STATIONS

Carlisle is 6 miles (9.5km) east of Burgh by Sands on Hadrian's Cycleway (National Route 72).

BIKE HIRE

None locally.

FURTHER INFORMATION

- To view or print National Cycle Network routes, visit www.sustrans.org.uk

SOLWAY COAST FROM BURGH BY SANDS

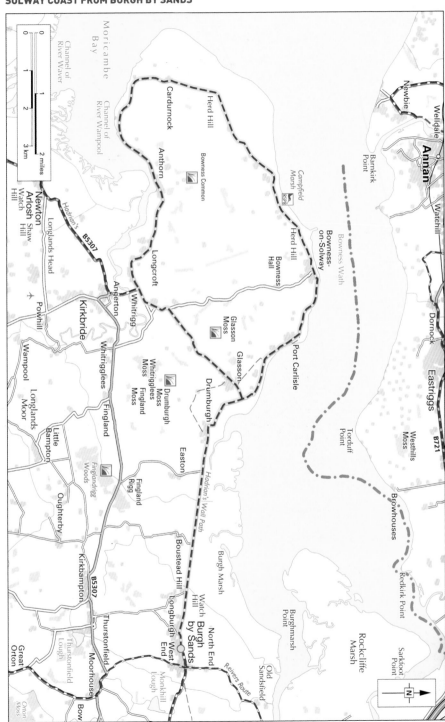

Campfield Marsh
RSPB reserve

- Maps for this area are available to buy from www.sustransshop.co.uk
- Solway Coast Tourist Information: 01697 333055; www.solwaycoastaonb.org.uk
- Hadrian's Wall: www.hadrians-wall.org

ROUTE DESCRIPTION

Head west out of Burgh by Sands, following the long straight road bordering Burgh Marsh, and go through Drumburgh. Take the first left turn to go through Glasson, then go left again at the next junction. Turn right and keep straight ahead, following the blue signs for Hadrian's Cycleway (National Route 72) to Anthorn. Continue right around the Cardurnock peninsula to Bowness-on-Solway, then back to your start point in Burgh by Sands. Turning

right directly to Bowness-on-Solway before Whitrigg shortens the ride by 8 miles (13km).

NEARBY CYCLE ROUTES

Hadrian's Cycleway (National Route 72) continues along the Cumbrian coast through Silloth, Maryport and Whitehaven to Ravenglass. From Burgh bySands, the route goes through Carlisle on its way to the remains of Hadrian's Wall and the eastern end of the route at South Shields. Hadrian's Cycleway is 174 miles (280km) long in total.

A pack of five OS map-based day-ride leaflets on cycling around the Solway Coast is available from the Solway Coast Discovery Centre in Silloth (016973 31944).

NORTH YORKSHIRE MOORS & SEA – SCARBOROUGH TO WHITBY

The Scarborough & Whitby Railway, which operated from 1885 until 1965, allowed tourists to explore the rugged coastline between the two towns on the edge of North York Moors National Park. Now you can cycle, walk and horse-ride along most of its original length, enjoying spectacular coastal scenery. There are numerous pit stops and diversions, too, including picturesque Robin Hood's Bay, with its smuggling past and fossil-hunting beach, and the incredible Peak Alum Works at Ravenscar.

Scarborough, Britain's first seaside resort, has two sandy beaches, with safe swimming areas and a Sea Life centre. The ruins of the medieval castle on the rocky headland give a good view of the place. At the other end of the ride, the impressive Larpool Viaduct leads you across the River Esk into the bustling, history-filled streets of Whitby. It was from here that James Cook set out on his first seafaring adventure in 1746. The direct way to the dramatically set ruins of Whitby Abbey lies a little further back, along the railway path at Hawsker. There's an excellent youth hostel next to the Abbey and other places to stay overnight in the town if you want to cycle back down the coast the following day.

ROUTE INFORMATION
National Route: 1
Start: Safe Ways Park (behind Sainsbury's supermarket on Falsgrave Road), Scarborough.
Finish: Whitby Harbour or Whitby Abbey.
Distance: 21 miles (34km). Shorter option: from Scarborough to Robin Hood's Bay 15 miles (24km).
Grade: Medium.
Surface: The railway track bed does have some rough sections and the odd puddle. The on-road sections are tarmac.
Hills: None, but it's a steady climb over the summits at Ravenscar and Hawsker.

YOUNG & INEXPERIENCED CYCLISTS
All traffic-free, apart from short on-road sections in Scalby, Ravenscar, Robin Hood's Bay and Whitby. There are toucan crossings for getting safely over the A165 at Burniston and the A171 at Hawsker.

REFRESHMENTS
- Lots of choice in Scarborough, Robin Hood's Bay and Whitby.
- Station House Tearoom, Cloughton.

SCARBOROUGH

- Hayburn Wyke Inn, Hayburn Wyke.
- Foxcliffe Tearooms, Ravenscar.
- Tearoom at Trailways, Hawsker.
- Abbey Tearooms, Abbey House YHA hostel, next door to Whitby Abbey.

THINGS TO SEE & DO
Scarborough:
- **Scarborough Castle:** exhibitions covering 2,500 years of history; tearoom;

Robin Hood's Bay

Larpool Viaduct, near Whitby

Map labels (WHITBY)

N
NORTH TERRACE
UPGANG LANE
HUDSON ST
AVENUE
CRESCENT
SPRING VALE
KIRKHAM RD
CHUBB HILL RD
Pannett Park
ST HILDA'S TERR
BAGDALE
MEADOW FIELDS
A174
SPRING HILL
WINDSOR TERRACE
LARGBOURNE RD
Whitby Station
River Esk
CLIFF ST
PIER ROAD
KHYBER PASS
CHURCH STREET
THE ROPERY
Whitby Abbey

WHITBY

01723 372451;
www.english-heritage.org.uk/scarborough
- **Peasholm Park, North Bay area:** parkland, boating lake and cafes;
  www.peasholmpark.com
- **Sea Life and Marine Sanctuary, Scalby Mills:** many creatures of the deep in recreated natural habitats; 0871 423 2110;
  www.sealife.co.uk

Ravenscar:
- **Coastal Centre & Peak Alum Works:** the centre explains the history of the nearby remains of the alum works, and has

ammonites and other fossils for which the area is also renowned; 01723 870423;
www.nationaltrust.org.uk

Robin Hood's Bay:
- **Old Coastguard Station:** information and education facilities; 01723 870423;
  www.nationaltrust.org.uk

Whitby:
- **Whitby Abbey:** Gothic ruin with museum and visitor centre; 01947 603568;
  www.english-heritage.org.uk/whitby
- **Captain Cook Memorial Museum:** 17th-century house on the harbour where the young James Cook lodged as an apprentice; 01947 601900; www.cookmuseumwhitby.co.uk

TRAIN STATIONS
Scarborough; Whitby.

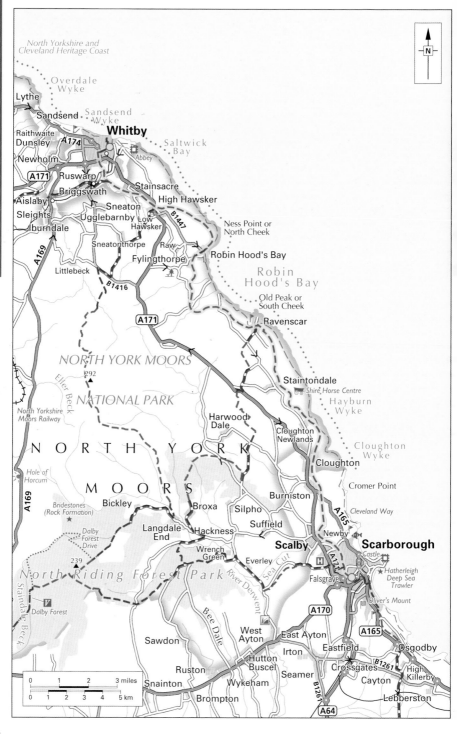

North Yorkshire and
Cleveland Heritage Coast

North Yorkshire Moors & Sea — Scarborough to Whitby map

Places shown: Overdale Wyke, Lythe, Sandsend, Sandsend Wyke, Raithwaite, Dunsley, **Whitby**, Newholm, Saltwick Bay, Aislaby, Ruswarp, Briggswath, Stainsacre, Sleights, Sneaton, High Hawsker, Iburndale, Ugglebarnby, Low Hawsker, Littlebeck, Sneatonthorpe, Raw, Ness Point or North Cheek, Fylingthorpe, Robin Hood's Bay, Robin Hood's Bay, Old Peak or South Cheek, **NORTH YORK MOORS**, 292, Ravenscar, **NATIONAL PARK**, North Yorkshire Moors Railway, Eller Beck, Staintondale, Shire Horse Centre, Hayburn Wyke, Harwood Dale, Cloughton Newlands, Cloughton Wyke, **NORTH YORK**, Hole of Horcum, Cloughton, **MOORS**, Bridestones (Rock Formation), Bickley, Broxa, Silpho, Burniston, Cromer Point, Cleveland Way, A169, Suffield, Newby, Langdale End, Hackness, Scalby, **Scarborough**, North Riding Forest Park, 239, Wrench Green, Everley, Sea Cut, Castle, Hatherleigh Deep Sea Trawler, Standale Beck, Dalby Forest, Falsgrave, Oliver's Mount, Sawdon, West Ayton, East Ayton, Irton, Eastfield, Osgodby, Ruston, Hutton Buscel, Seamer, Crossgates, Cayton, High Killerby, Snainton, Wykeham, Brompton, Lebberston

Roads: A174, A171, A169, B1447, B1416, A171, A165, A171, A170, A165, B1261, B1261, A64

Scale: 0 1 2 3 miles / 0 1 2 3 4 5 km

St Hilda's Abbey, Whitby

BIKE HIRE

- Trailways, The Old Railway Station, Hawsker: 01947 820207; www.trailways.info

FURTHER INFORMATION

- To view or print National Cycle Network routes, visit www.sustrans.org.uk
- Maps for this area are available to buy from www.sustransshop.co.uk
- Scarborough Tourist Information: 01723 383636; www.discoveryorkshirecoast.com
- Information point at Trailways, Hawsker: 01947 820207; www.trailways.info
- Whitby Tourist Information: 01947 602124; www.yorkshire.com
- Scarborough to Whitby Railway: www.friendsoftheoldrailway.org

ROUTE DESCRIPTION

From Safe Ways Park (a children's play area), go under the road bridge and onto the railway path. Keep following the blue signs for National Route 1 all the way to Whitby. At Hayburn Wyke, where there used to be a small railway station, a short walk across a field leads to a quiet bay.

To reach Whitby Abbey directly, leave the railway path at the cycle hire centre in the former railway station at Hawsker, carefully cross the A171 and follow Hawsker Lane.

Whitby Abbey and old town steps

Otherwise, the railway path leads you onto the Larpool Viaduct high above the River Esk and down into Whitby town. Use the ramp just before the end of the path and Bagdale Road to reach the harbour.

NEARBY CYCLE ROUTES

This route is part of the 110-mile (177km) Moor to Sea Cycle Route linking Scarborough, Pickering, Whitby and Great Ayton (www.moortoseacycle.net).

National Route 1 goes through Scarborough town centre to the South Bay and on to Bridlington. Running inland from Whitby up the Esk Valley to Great Ayton and all the way to Barnard Castle is Regional Route 52. This forms part of the Walney to Wear & Whitby (W2W) coast-to-coast cycle route.

CLEVELAND COAST – REDCAR TO SALTBURN-BY-SEA

The small, easy-going seaside resorts of Redcar and Saltburn sit on a stretch of Cleveland coastline running from the mouth of the River Tees to the foot of the Cleveland Hills. Rocky reefs give way to unbroken sand and shingle beach, where fishing cobles (boats) are drawn up. The section of National Route 1 that links the two towns is largely flat and traffic-free.

Built around its racecourse, Redcar is less well known as the home of the world's oldest surviving lifeboat, *Zetland*, which is displayed in the museum of that name – the town's lifeboat men who manned *Zetland* back in the early 1800s saved over 500 lives.

Attractive Marske-by-the-Sea village has a Captain Cook connection in the churchyard, and during World War I it was a training camp for the Royal Flying Corps, producing many flying aces. The now-disappeared airfield was where the *Biggles* books were written by Captain W. E. Johns.

Saltburn was a popular bathing spot in Victorian times, with visitors to the town using the water-balanced cliff lift to reach the pleasure pier directly below it. You can enjoy both before returning to Redcar, either by catching a train or cycling back along the same route.

ROUTE INFORMATION
National Route: 1
Start: Redcar Central train station.
Finish: Saltburn train station.
Distance: 6 miles (9.5km). Shorter options: Redcar to Marske train station 3.5 miles (5.5km); Marske train station to Saltburn train station 3 miles (5km).

Grade: Easy, but will feel harder in a stiff coastal breeze.
Surface: Tarmac on-road, and tarmac or compacted stone dust off-road.
Hills: None, except a short, steep climb in Saltburn.

YOUNG & INEXPERIENCED CYCLISTS
Not all traffic-free path, but the linking road sections in Redcar, Marske and Saltburn are traffic-calmed, with toucan crossings on Coast Road. If cycling back from Marske to Redcar,

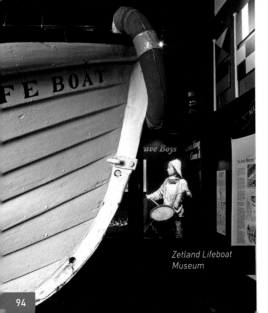

Zetland Lifeboat Museum

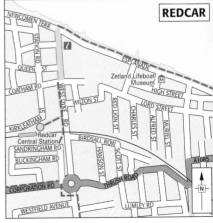

Marske beach and Cliff House

ou can use the pavement opposite as you turn ight onto Marske High Street, heading for the cyclepath and toucan crossing a little further on.

REFRESHMENTS

- Lots of choice in Redcar, Marske and Saltburn.
- Pacitto's Ice Cream Parlour, Redcar.
- Stray Cafe, Coast Road, Redcar.
- Ship Inn, Marske.

- Signals and Virgos (coffee shop and bistro), Saltburn.
- The Ship Inn, Saltburn, on the A174.

THINGS TO SEE & DO

- **Zetland Lifeboat Museum, Redcar:** replica fisherman's cottage and displays of local maritime history, as well as the 1802 lifeboat; 01642 494311; www.redcar-cleveland.gov.uk/museums
- **St Germain's Churchyard, Marske:** historic churchyard where Captain Cook's father was buried in 1779.
- **Cliff Lift in Saltburn:** oldest of its type in Britain; seasonal operation; 01287 622528

TRAIN STATIONS

Redcar Central; Redcar East;
Marske; Saltburn.

BIKE HIRE

None locally.

FURTHER INFORMATION

- To view or print National Cycle Network routes, visit www.sustrans.org.uk

Saltburn Cliff Lift and
Victorian pier

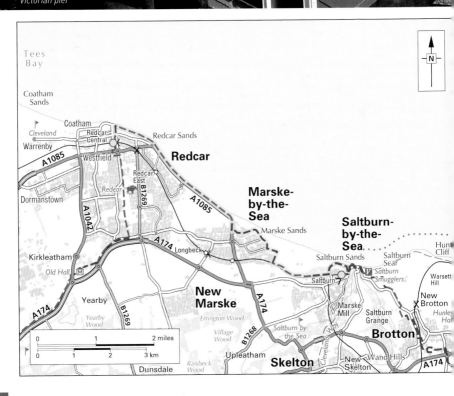

Tees
Bay

Coatham
Sands

Cleveland
Warrenby

Coatham
Redcar
Central

Redcar Sands

Redcar

Westfield

A1085

Redcar
East

Redcar

B1269

A1085

**Marske-
by-the-
Sea**

Dormanstown

A1042

A174

Longbeck

Marske Sands

**Saltburn-
by-the-
Sea**

Saltburn Sands

Hunt
Cliff

Saltburn
Scar

Saltburn
Smugglers

Warsett
Hill

Kirkleatham

Old Hall

Yearby

Yearby
Wood

B1269

**New
Marske**

Errington Wood

A174

Saltburn

Marske
Mill

Saltburn
Grange

New
Brotton

Hunley
Hall

A174

Village
Wood

B1268

Saltburn by
the Sea

Cleveland Way

Brotton

Dunsdale

Raisbeck
Wood

Upleatham

Skelton

New
Skelton

Wand Hills

A174

0   1   2 miles

0   1   2   3 km

Maps for this area are available to buy from www.sustransshop.co.uk

Redcar Tourist Information: 01642 471921; www.visitredcarandcleveland.co.uk

Saltburn Tourist Information: 01287 622422; www.visitredcarandcleveland.co.uk

North East England Tourist Information: www.visitnortheastengland.com

ROUTE DESCRIPTION

Redcar Central train station is right on National Route 1. Come out of the station and turn left, heading north along West Dyke Road. You can either follow the blue signed route or continue along West Dyke Road until you get to Coast Road. Turn right and stay on the traffic-free path all the way to Marske. The blue signed route continues along quiet roads through the village to reach another traffic-free section running alongside the railway from Windy Hill Lane.

Follow the traffic-free route through the allotments to meet Milton Street and the way into Saltburn. Turn left into Marine Parade and follow the route all the way round to turn right into Milton Street again. Saltburn station is on the left (behind the Somerfield store).

Alternatively, if you would like to take a closer look at the Victorian pier, turn left away from Milton Street, carefully make the bendy descent to the foreshore and bear left.

To return to the town centre, continue cycling round past the pier to reach a steep and stony bridleway track called the Donkey Path. On your way back, you may decide that it would be better to dismount and walk your bike up the steep track.

NEARBY CYCLE ROUTES

National Route 1 continues mainly on-road from Saltburn via Skinningrove to Staithes harbour. From Redcar, Route 1 goes inland to Middlesbrough on the River Tees.

Visit www.doitbycycle.com for more Tees Valley rides and information.

See also the North Yorkshire Moors & Sea ride between Scarborough and Whitby (page 90), and the Tees Bridges Ride (page 98).

TEES BRIDGES – FROM THE TEES BARRAGE

The Tees is one of Northern England's great rivers, which once formed the boundary between the historic counties of Yorkshire and County Durham. Near the sea, it has for centuries been an important commercial waterway, undergoing many changes since the early 1800s to make it deeper and more navigable. This circular ride makes good use of a riverside section of National Route 1, and follows the river between the Tees Barrage and the famous Transporter Bridge (not disassembled and sent to Arizona, as in the *Auf Wiedersehen Pet* television show), blending industrial heritage and Tees Valley regeneration with the natural world. The wildlife reserve and discovery park at Saltholme, with a state-of-the-art visitor centre, is Britain's newest and largest RSPB site, and is free to cyclists (and those arriving on foot or by bus). Bear in mind that the Transporter Bridge is closed on Sunday mornings until 2pm for maintenance; it costs 60p for pedestrians with bicycles.

ROUTE INFORMATION

National Route: 1
Start: The Tees Barrage.
Finish: The Tees Barrage.
Distance: 10 miles (16km). Shorter option: from the Tees Barrage to Newport Bridge and back 3 miles (5km).
Grade: Easy.
Surface: Tarmac and track to the visitor centre

at Saltholme nature reserve, which is liable to have some surface water in wet weather and can be rough at times.
Hills: None.

YOUNG & INEXPERIENCED CYCLISTS

All flat and traffic-free, apart from either side of the Transporter Bridge, and Port Clarence Road, which you need to cross to reach the Saltholme nature reserve track. Extra care should be taken here.

REFRESHMENTS

- The Watersports Centre and The Talpore pub at the Tees Barrage.
- Visitor centre cafe, Saltholme nature reserve

THINGS TO SEE & DO

- **The Tees Barrage:** 'white water' water sports centre for canoeing and kayaking; 01642 678000
- **RSPB Saltholme nature reserve:** 1,000-acre reserve, adventure playground and visitor centre; 01642 546625; www.rspb.org.uk
- **Transporter Bridge:** the second largest of its type remaining in the world; 01642 247563
- **Teesaurus Park:** collection of steel dinosaur on the south bank of the River Tees.
- **Captain Cook Birthplace Museum, Marton:**

The Tees Barrage

tells the story of one of the world's greatest
navigators and mariners; 01642 311211;
www.captcook-ne.co.uk

TRAIN STATIONS
Thornaby; Middlesbrough.

BIKE HIRE
None locally.

FURTHER INFORMATION
- To view or print National Cycle Network
  routes, visit www.sustrans.org.uk

Birdwatchers at
RSPB Saltholme

Transporter Bridge
over the River Tees

- Maps for this area are available to buy from www.sustransshop.co.uk
- Stockton Tourist Information: 01642 528130; www.visitstockton.co.uk
- Middlesbrough Tourist Information: 01642 729900; www.visitmiddlesbrough.com

ROUTE DESCRIPTION

There are on-road cycle lanes from Thornaby and Middlesbrough stations to the start of this ride. From the Tees Barrage car park, head down to the Barrage and turn left onto the traffic-free path running parallel to the north bank of the river. Follow this path along the river, past the Portrack Marshes nature reserve, under the A19 and then under Newport Bridge. Follow the path as it heads up to the A1032, turn left at the top onto the cycle route, taking you north towards Portrack. At the roundabout, bear right, following signs for Haverton Hill and Port Clarence. Continue on this traffic-free path to Port Clarence Road.

About halfway along the roadside path to Port Clarence, look out for the sign to the Saltholme nature reserve – take extra care crossing the road. The gate on the track leading to the visitor centre is open from 10am until 4.40pm (3.40pm from October to March). Leaving the reserve, return to the cyclepath and turn left to the Transporter Bridge. On the other side, turn right to join National Route 1 and follow it and the River Tees upstream, passing the Teesaurus Park and the River Tees nature reserve, all the way back to your starting point. The new Infinity Bridge is a little further upstream and worth a closer look.

NEARBY CYCLE ROUTES

You can follow National Route 1 to the North Sea coast at Redcar (see the Redcar to Saltburn ride on page 94). Across the River Tees from Middlesbrough, Route 1 is intersected by Route 14 coming from the centre of Stockton-on-Tees and heading out through Billingham to Cowpen Bewley Woodland Park.

Visit www.doitbycycle.com for more Tees Valley rides and information.

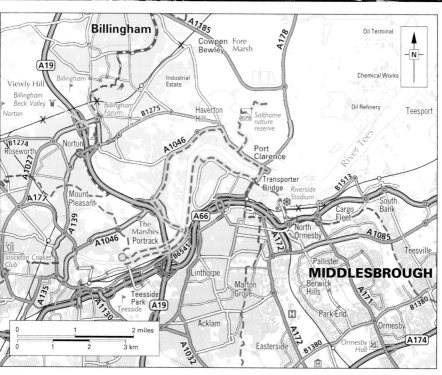

ROKER BEACH TO BEAMISH MUSEUM

This ride begins where most people who do the Sea-to-Sea Cycle Route (C2C) finish their 136-mile (219km) adventure, on the seafront at Roker in Sunderland. You're soon passing along the regenerated north bank of the River Wear, where shipbuilding and deep coal mining have been replaced by splendid landmarks such as the National Glass Centre and the Stadium of Light, home of the Black Cats (Sunderland AFC). Look out for hidden sculptural hints of the new city's industrial past, once described as the biggest shipbuilding town in the world: a giant nut and bolt, a fragment of a house suddenly abandoned and a metal tree that casts the shadow of a shipyard crane.

After about 6 miles (9.5km) of riverbank, the route climbs up to a wildfowl and wetlands centre. It then continues into Washington, where it joins the disused railway that carried iron ore from Spain and further afield to feed the furnaces of Consett steelworks, and then took the finished steel away. The railway path was one of Sustrans' earliest projects, started in 1987, and included many firsts, such as the renowned sculpture trail. Look out for the *Lambton Worm* by Andy Goldsworthy, David Kemp's *King Coal*, which looks like a giant chess piece, and the remarkably docile *Cows* created by Sally Matthews at Beamish.

The route climbs steadily after Washington to Beamish – imagine 900 tonnes of iron ore being hauled up this bank by two huge steam engines, one pulling, the other pushing from the back. The track fell silent in 1984 after it performed its last job of taking away the steelworks bit by bit. Now it's a leafy, shaded cutting. You will have reached journey's end when you see the twisted and tangled remains of old JCB parts, now reformed to help keep the grass down, adjacent to the ramp that leads to Beamish Museum.

Roker pier

ROUTE INFORMATION
National Routes: 7, 1
Start: The 'C' sculpture, Roker seafront, near the pier.
Finish: Eden Place picnic area, Beamish.
Distance: 15 miles (24km).
Grade: Medium. There is a gradual climb on the disused railway, with some short, steep slopes on the early section beside Sunderland Enterprise Park.
Surface: Tarmac and stone-dust path.
Hills: None.

YOUNG & INEXPERIENCED CYCLISTS
Some minor road crossings on the outskirts of Sunderland, but entirely traffic-free from Washington onwards, though take care crossing the road next to the Arts Centre.

'Shadows in Another Light' sculpture

Sunderland AFC stadium

STADIUM OF LIGHT

REFRESHMENTS
- Snowgoose Cafe, Sunderland Marina.
- National Glass Centre, Sunderland.
- Cafe bar at the Washington Arts Centre.
- Wheatsheaf pub, Barley Mow.
- Shepherd and Shepherdess pub, Beamish.

THINGS TO SEE & DO
- **National Glass Centre, Sunderland:** exhibitions and studio; 0191 515 5555; www.nationalglasscentre.com
- **St Peter's Church, Wearmouth:** one of the UK's earliest stone-built churches, overlooking the River Wear; 0191 516 0135; www.wearmouth-jarrow.org.uk
- **Washington Wetland Centre:** mix of wetland, woodland and wildlife reserve; 0191 416 5454; www.wwt.org.uk
- **Beamish Museum:** working museum recreating how people in the north of England lived and worked in the early 1800s and 1900s; 0191 370 4000; www.beamish.org.uk

TRAIN STATIONS
Sunderland; Chester-le-Street.

BIKE HIRE
- **Cycle World, Sunderland:** 0191 565 8188
- **Peter Darke Cycles, Sunderland:** 0191 510 8155

FURTHER INFORMATION
- To view or print National Cycle Network routes, visit www.sustrans.org.uk
- Maps for this area are available to buy from www.sustransshop.co.uk
- **Sunderland Tourist Information:** 0191 553 2000; www.visitsunderland.com

ROUTE DESCRIPTION
With the sea on your left, leave the 'C' sculpture

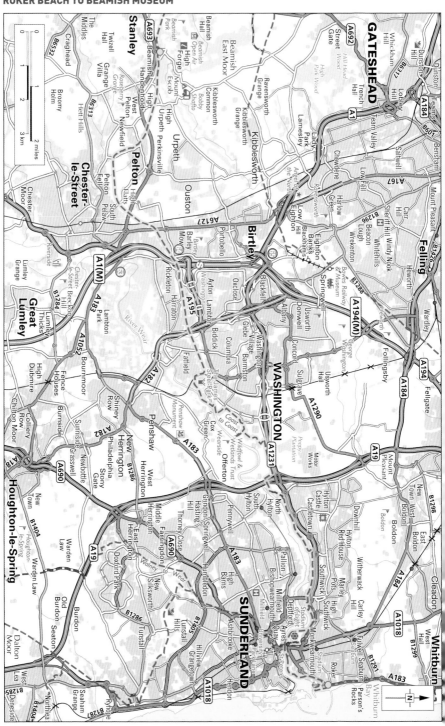

Scenes of bygone days at Beamish Museum

on Roker seafront, following blue C2C National Route 7 signs to the mouth of the River Wear and round behind Sunderland Marina. Continue along the riverbank, passing the National Glass Centre and Sunderland University, and eventually going under the Wearmouth Bridge. The route then curves around past the Stadium of Light and on through some industrial estates and Sunderland Enterprise Park, occasionally rising and falling. After approximately 4 miles (6.5km), the route drops back down to the riverside at North Hylton, passing under the massive concrete A19 bridge. Thereafter, you turn right and follow a field-edge stone-dust path for approximately 1 mile (1.6km), to enter some woodland that leads to the Washington Wetland Centre. You will then drop to the riverside again, at Cox Green, and back up into

James Steel Country Park. Leave the country park via a stone arched railway bridge and enter sharp right into a small plantation that connects with the railway path at Fatfield. Take care at the road crossing next to the Arts Centre and follow the cyclepath and sculpture trail for the next 7 miles (11km), crossing over the old Great North Road and then the East Coast mainline railway, and then skirting around Chester-le-Street to begin the steady climb to Beamish. The route goes past the entrance gates to Beamish Museum.

NEARBY CYCLE ROUTES

This route is part of the renowned Sea-to-Sea Cycle Route (C2C) between West Cumbria and Tyne/Wearside. National Route 1 takes you up the coast to South Shields and the River Tyne.

DERWENT WALK & GIBSIDE FROM SWALWELL

This circular ride offers a long but gentle pull up the old railway line from the River Tyne towards Consett, before turning near Rowlands Gill and swooping back downhill through Derwenthaugh Country Park, once the site of a massive coke works. The Derwent Walk was one of the first conversions of a disused railway from 'rail-to-trail' for walking and cycling in the UK. Now, it is a leafy, shaded corridor, hidden from the elements. Watch out for red kites circling high overhead. Reintroduced to the Derwent Valley comparatively recently, these birds have been a great success, as has the reclamation of the coke works with the creation of plantations, grassy meadows and swan-inhabited ponds. At Rowlands Gill, you'll cross a viaduct giving panoramic views of the wider area, including the tall Column of Liberty rising out of the woodland, the ruins of Gibside Hall and the remaining chapel amid the pleasure grounds. These were created by the Bowes-Lyon family – the late Queen Mother was its best-known member – from the proceeds of coal mining.

The Orangery,
Gibside Hall

DERWENT WALK & GIBSIDE FROM SWALWELL

Derwent Country Park

ROUTE INFORMATION
National Route: 14
Start: Swalwell Visitor Centre (beside Blaydon Rugby Football Ground).
Finish: Swalwell Visitor Centre.
Distance: 8 miles (13km).
Grade: Easy.
Surface: Mixture of stone-dust path on the disused railway and sealed grit surface in the country park.
Hills: None, although there is a gentle uphill gradient on the disused railway, and a slightly steeper descent through the country park.

YOUNG & INEXPERIENCED CYCLISTS
Entirely traffic-free, except for the last road crossing in front of the rugby club at the finish and the entrance into Gibside.

REFRESHMENTS
- Lots of choice in the Swalwell area and at Rowlands Gill.
- Tearoom at Gibside, near Rowlands Gill.
- Golden Lion pub, Winlaton Mill.

THINGS TO SEE & DO
- Swalwell Visitor Centre, Gateshead: serves the end of the Derwent Walk Country Park, with displays and information; 0191 414 2106; www.visitnewcastlegateshead.com
- Thornley Woodlands Centre, Rowlands Gill: interpretative centre, serving the woodlands of the Derwent Walk Country Park and providing information on red kites and other points of interest; 01207 545212; www.visitnewcastlegateshead.com
- Gibside, near Rowlands Gill: stunning 18th-century landscape 'forest' garden; 01207 541820; www.nationaltrust.org.uk

TRAIN STATIONS
Metro Centre; Blaydon.

BIKE HIRE
- Newburn Activity Centre, Newburn: 0191 264 0014
- Whickham Thorns Activity Centre, Dunston: 0191 433 5767

FURTHER INFORMATION
- To view or print National Cycle Network routes, visit www.sustrans.org.uk
- Maps for this area are available to buy from www.sustransshop.co.uk

Derwenthaugh
Country Park

- **Gateshead Tourist Information:**
  0191 478 4222;
  www.visitnewcastlegateshead.com

ROUTE DESCRIPTION

On leaving Swalwell Visitor Centre, pick up the stone-dust cycle path signed towards Consett.

After 2 miles (3km), cross a viaduct and then travel a further 1.5 miles (2.5km) before entering Rowlands Gill. Pass through an entrance gate and stile to join a roadside pavement path leading past a garage forecourt before heading left down the B6314 towards Gibside. Pay close attention as you cross over

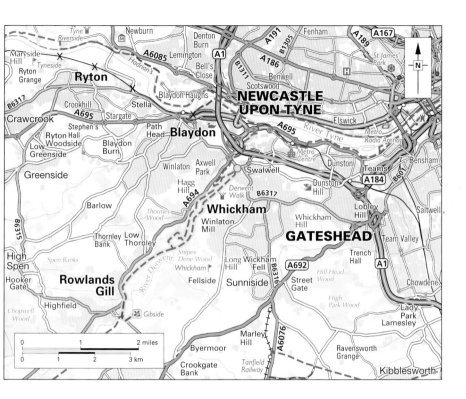

the narrow road bridge at the bottom of the bank. The entrance to Gibside will then be on your left.

To return, leave Gibside, following the same route back through Rowlands Gill onto the railway path and down to the viaduct. Immediately after you have crossed the viaduct, look to your left for an alternative signed route, which leads you down through Derwenthaugh Country Park. You will pass by the river, ponds and a weir, tennis courts, a cricket club and then back alongside the river before going under a road bridge.

Immediately after the bridge, look for a right-hand turn leading you over a humped bridge into a small housing estate and out onto the main road opposite the rugby club, which is next to the point where you started. Be careful crossing this road, even though it

has a sheltered island in the middle, especially if cycling in a group. Alternatively, you can cut straight through to the Swalwell Visitor Centre from the cricket club.

NEARBY CYCLE ROUTES

This route takes in the lower reaches of National Route 14, which forms part of the Sea-to-Sea Cycle Route (C2C) from Consett to Tyneside. There you can continue along the south side of the River Tyne on the Keelman's Way to central Gateshead and the bridges across to Newcastle.

By crossing the river earlier at Scotswood, you can link to Hadrian's Cycleway (Route 72), which follows the north bank of the Tyne through central Newcastle to Tynemouth and the North Sea coast beyond.

SOUTER TO ST MARY'S

This ride visits two North Sea lighthouses, one to the south and one to the north of the River Tyne estuary. They are linked via the Shields Ferry, which sails between South Shields and North Shields, and also by a route past Tynemouth Priory and Castle.

Souter Lighthouse, on the coastline between South Shields and Sunderland, is the world's first electric lighthouse, with fantastic views over Marsden Bay. Look out for the nesting seabirds on cliffs and stacks, and visit the tearoom serving delicious local specialities. The lighthouse is located on Lizard Point at Marsden, but takes its name from Souter Point, 1 mile (1.6km) to the south. Opened in 1871, the lighthouse was built due to the dangerous reefs in the surrounding area.

St Mary's Lighthouse is on St Mary's Island, just north of Whitley Bay, a small island linked to the mainland by a short concrete causeway that is submerged at high tide. While it no longer functions as a lighthouse, it is easily accessible (when the tide is out) and is open to visitors. It has a small museum, a visitor centre and a shop. Both the lighthouse and the adjacent keepers' cottages were built in 1898.

ROUTE INFORMATION
National Routes: 1, 72
Start: Souter Lighthouse, but do check which way the wind is blowing – a headwind can ruin this ride!
Finish: St Mary's Lighthouse.
Distance: 11 miles (17.5km).

Souter Lighthouse

Grade: Fairly easy with no strenuous climbs.
Surface: Tarmac.
Hills: Very few; some short, steep banks.

YOUNG & INEXPERIENCED CYCLISTS
A pleasant mixture of traffic-free paths and quiet roads makes this ride a good choice for families and novices.

REFRESHMENTS
- Cafe at Souter Lighthouse.
- Marsden Grotto pub.
- Kopper Kettle cafe (Westoe Road), South Shields.
- North Shields Fish Quay and market, selling fresh fish as well as fish and chips.
- Cafe in Tynemouth Priory.
- Lots of choice in Tynemouth, Cullercoats and Whitley Bay.

THINGS TO SEE & DO
- Tynemouth Priory: medieval Benedictine priory; www.english-heritage.org.uk
- Souter Lighthouse: www.nationaltrust.org.uk
- Blue Reef Aquarium, Tynemouth: includes seahorses, sharks, giant octopus, frogs and otters; 0191 258 1031; www.bluereefaquarium.co.uk

Percy Chapel,
Tynemouth Priory

Nesting gulls at
Lizard Point

- St Mary's Lighthouse, St Mary's Island:
  0191 200 8650;
  www.friendsofstmarysisland.co.uk

FERRY
Shields Ferry runs roughly every 30 minutes:
0191 454 8183; www.nexus.org.uk/ferry

METRO STATIONS
Only folding bikes can be taken on the Metro.
Tyne Dock (green line) is the nearest station to
Souter Lighthouse; Whitley Bay (yellow line) to
St Mary's Lighthouse.

BIKE HIRE
- South Tyneside Cycle Hire: 0191 455 6313;
  www.visitnortheastengland.com
- Cyclops, North Shields: adapted bikes for the
  disabled; 07974 720002; www.cyclopsnt.org

FURTHER INFORMATION
- To view or print National Cycle Network
  routes, visit www.sustrans.org.uk
- Maps for this area are available to buy from
  www.sustransshop.co.uk
- Northeast England Tourist Information: 0844
  249 5090; www.visitnortheastengland.com

ROUTE DESCRIPTION
From Souter Lighthouse, ride north on National
Route 1 using the cycle lane on the shared-use
footway. You will shortly pass Marsden Rock.
Cross over the roundabout in front of the New
Crown pub to the playing field. Follow signs for
National Route 1 and the pedestrian ferry.

After a yellow gate, turn right (using the road
or footway) and then turn immediately left up
Sea Way. Cross over Salisbury Place and use
the traffic-free Route 1 path adjacent to Erskine
Road. Cross Westoe Road and continue on
Route 1, passing under the Metro and road
bridges and bearing to the right past Wickes
DIY store. Continue until you reach the Shields
Ferry terminal. There is a bike rack situated on
the rear lower deck. Leave the North Shields

ferry terminal and turn right along Clive Street,
following signs for National Route 72 and
Tynemouth/Whitley Bay. Bear right down
Liddell Street towards the North Shields Fish
Quay and market. After the New Dolphin pub,
turn right following signs on street lights for
Route 1. You then reach the *Old Buoys* artwork,
which celebrates the confluence of three
National Routes: 1, 10 and 72. Go through the
car park and onto the promenade, turning left.
In peak season, the promenade may be busy, so
be sure to warn pedestrians of your approach.
Turn left up a short but steep bank for stunning
views of Tynemouth Priory.

At the Gibraltar Rock pub, you may decide to
use the footway for the next couple of miles.
Cycle alongside the Whitley Bay Promenade,

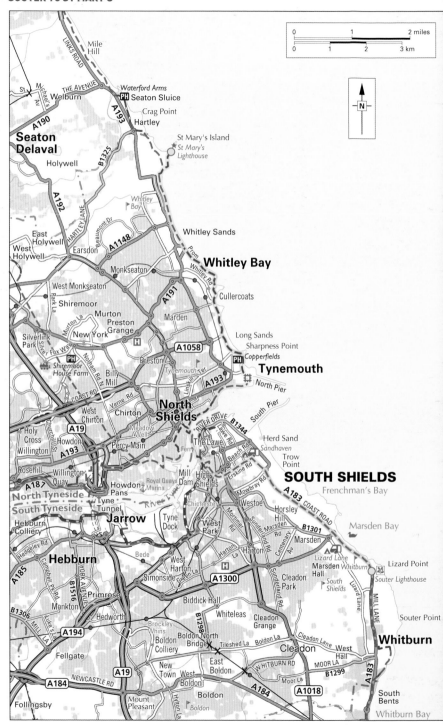

St Mary's Lighthouse

from where there are amazing views. Pass the Queen's Head pub and turn right down Norma Crescent after passing the tractors and boats in dry dock. There are excellent views of Tynemouth to the right, and on a clear day you can see Souter Lighthouse.

Turn left and rejoin the promenade route. Take care at a couple of road crossings that lead to the beach. Turn right off the promenade route onto the shared-use footway leading to St Mary's Lighthouse.

NEARBY CYCLE ROUTES

This route follows National Routes 72 and 1. Route 72 forms Hadrian's Cycleway, which stretches the length of Hadrian's Wall World Heritage Site from Glannaventa Roman Bath House in Ravenglass to Arbeia Roman Fort and Museum in South Shields. Route 72 also links with National Route 7, which forms part of the C2C, running from Workington and Whitehaven to Newcastle and Sunderland. The section of the ride that uses Route 1 is part of the Coast & Castles route from Newcastle to Edinburgh.

The Wylam Loop is a 20-mile (32km) ride from Newcastle to Gateshead via Wylam, with a shorter option going from Newburn to Wylam (see page 114).

TYNE RIVERSIDE – NEWBURN TO CORBRIDGE

In spite of this ride being on a section of Hadrian's Cycleway, it's more about the River Tyne and railway history. There is, though, the site of a Roman town to explore at the end.

The ride starts at the Newburn end of the Tyne Riverside Country Park, on the western outskirts of Newcastle. Newburn was the site of a battle between the English and the Scots during the time of the English Civil War – the odd cannon ball has been recovered from the river. The route travels via an old railway line along the north bank of the River Tyne and into the spectacular countryside of Tynedale. Along the way, you pass Wylam and the cottage where George Stephenson, the 'father of the railway', was born. To the west of Wylam is a mini-Tyne Bridge, an early prototype of the Sydney Harbour Bridge, now carefully restored in its original livery of mouse grey. The route continues on the south bank of the river to Prudhoe before crossing north again at Ovingham. Thereafter, it continues on minor country roads to reach rather quaint Corbridge, which grew from the Roman town of Corstopitum, a supply town for the troops on Hadrian's Wall.

ROUTE INFORMATION

National Route: 72
Start: Tyne Riverside Country Park Visitor Centre, Newburn.
Finish: Corbridge town square.
Distance: 12 miles (19.5km).
Grade: Easy for the first 10 miles (16km), then a climb up from the riverside into Corbridge.

Surface: Sealed surface cyclepath, followed by tarmac road.
Hills: None.

YOUNG & INEXPERIENCED CYCLISTS

Ideal for novices and families throughout the traffic-free section to Ovingham, but some care is required crossing the narrow Ovingham

Single-track bridge over the River Tyne

George Stephenson's cottage, Wylam

Bridge (you may want to walk along the footway). Care is also needed on the minor road to Corbridge, especially at the junction with the B road leading into the town centre.

REFRESHMENTS

- Keelman Pub & Big Lamp Brewery, Newburn.
- Tearoom at George Stephenson's Birthplace, Wylam.
- Lots of choice in Wylam, Prudhoe and Corbridge.

THINGS TO SEE & DO

- **George Stephenson's Birthplace, Wylam:** miner's cottage furnished to reflect domestic living in 1781, the year Stephenson was born; 01661 853457; www.nationaltrust.org.uk
- **Wylam Railway Museum:** displays showing the importance of Wylam in railway development and the work of famous local pioneers George Stephenson, Timothy Hackworth and William Hedley; 01661 852174

- **Corbridge Roman Site (Hadrian's Wall),** half a mile (0.8km) northwest of Corbridge following Hadrian's Cycleway: walk along the main street of this Roman garrison town, flanked by the remains of granaries, markets, workshops and temples; 01434 632349; www.english-heritage.org.uk

TRAIN STATIONS

Blaydon; Wylam; Prudhoe; Stocksfield; Corbridge.

BIKE HIRE

- **Newburn Activity Centre, Newburn:** 0191 264 0014

FURTHER INFORMATION

- To view or print National Cycle Network routes, visit www.sustrans.org.uk

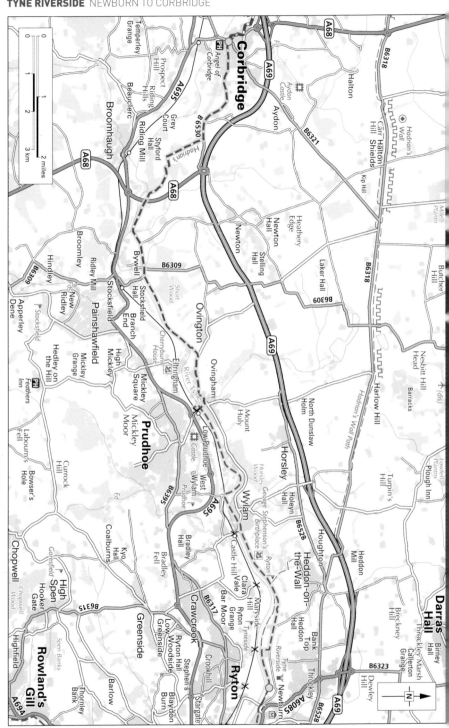

Roman remains at Corbridge

- Maps for this area are available to buy from www.sustransshop.co.uk
- Newcastle Tourist Information: 0191 277 8000; www.visitnewcastlegateshead.com
- Corbridge Tourist Information: 01434 632815; www.thisiscorbridge.co.uk
- Hexham Tourist Information: 01434 652220
- Hadrian's Wall: www.hadrians-wall.org

ROUTE DESCRIPTION

Turn right out of the visitor centre car park at Tyne Riverside Country Park in Newburn. With the river on your left, pass the boat slipway and toilets on your right. At the next junction, follow the blue Hadrian's Cycleway signed path (National Route 72) that swings away from the river and leads you to the entrance to the railway path on your left. Follow this route for 2 miles (3km), passing the golf course on your right, all the way to George Stephenson's Birthplace cottage and on through Wylam itself. Continue over Points Bridge and keep following the signs to the right alongside the river, which lead you on to Prudhoe. When you reach the next visitor centre in Prudhoe, turn back to cross spectacular Ovingham Bridge (do take care on this narrow bridge – use the footway for safety). At the end of the bridge, turn left onto minor roads leading through to Bywell and then alongside the river to Corbridge.

Prudhoe Castle

NEARBY CYCLE ROUTES

This route forms part of Hadrian's Cycleway (National Route 72), running between Ravenglass in West Cumbria and South Shields (www.cycle-routes.org/hadrianscycleway).

See also www.hadrians-wall.org for additional cycle routes.

East of Newburn, near Blaydon, there's a link with Route 14 and the Derwent Walk ride (see page 106).

NORTHUMBERLAND COAST – ALNMOUTH TO DRURIDGE BAY

This coastal ride mixes the old with the new. It passes castles and fortifications from a violent past, fishing villages with just a few working boats left, and ends with a new country park, the legacy of opencast mining and sand extraction. Alnmouth self-evidently stands at the mouth of the River Aln, often commented on by rail travellers for its picture-postcard, pastel-coloured cottages with red pantile roofs. But, in fact, the mouth of the river has moved as a result of many years of flooding and tidal changes before forming the new channel during a storm on Christmas Day 1806, leaving the old harbour silted up and cut off.

On this ride, you'll be following a section of the Coast & Castles Cycle Route and making use of a purpose-built, field-edge path, which keeps you off the fast and busy road to Warkworth. Striking Warkworth Castle towers over the village, once a stronghold of the Percy family, whose lion emblem can be seen carved on many parts of the castle. Upstream, you can also visit the Hermitage via a short river ferry crossing. Elsewhere on the route you follow the lower reaches of the River Coquet, with its abundance of aquatic birdlife, until it flows out into the sea at the port and marina of Amble. Here, yachts and pleasure boats jostle with traditional fishing boats. You may linger a while and see a fresh catch of shellfish landed. South of the harbour, the route follows seaside tracks past cottages that once belonged to fishermen and coastguards, who watched for smugglers. Now, they're used as holiday homes. The last part of the route passes along the dunes heading south to the sweeping Druridge Bay, with its long, white sandy beaches created after controversial sand extraction and opencast mining operations.

Alnmouth beach and town

ROUTE INFORMATION
National Route: 1
Start: Alnmouth village centre.
Finish: Druridge Bay Visitor Centre.
Distance: 9 miles (14.5km).
Grade: Easy.
Surface: Tarmac roads, sealed surface off-road track and tarmac pavement path.
Hills: None.

YOUNG & INEXPERIENCED CYCLISTS
Take care leaving Alnmouth on the Hipsburn road and in Amble town centre.

REFRESHMENTS
- Lots of choice in Alnmouth, Warkworth and Amble.

THINGS TO SEE & DO
- **Warkworth Castle & Hermitage:** impressive, almost complete 14th-century hilltop fortress above the River Coquet; the late medieval Hermitage, partly made from

a cave, is half a mile (0.8km) away upriver; 01665 711423; www.english-heritage.org.uk
- **Northumberland Sea Bird Centre, Warkworth Harbour:** live CCTV footage of the seabird colony on the RSPB's Coquet Island nature reserve; coffee shop; 01665 710835; www.northumberlandseabirdcentre.co.uk
- **Druridge Bay Country Park, south of Amble:** beach, dunes, large freshwater lake, trails, visitor centre, coffee shop; 01670 760968

TRAIN STATIONS
Alnmouth; Acklington.

BIKE HIRE
- **Breeze Bikes, Coquet Enterprise Park, Amble:** 01665 710323; www.breezebikes.co.uk
- **Pedal Power, Amble:** 01665 713448; www.pedal-power.co.uk

FURTHER INFORMATION
- To view or print National Cycle Network

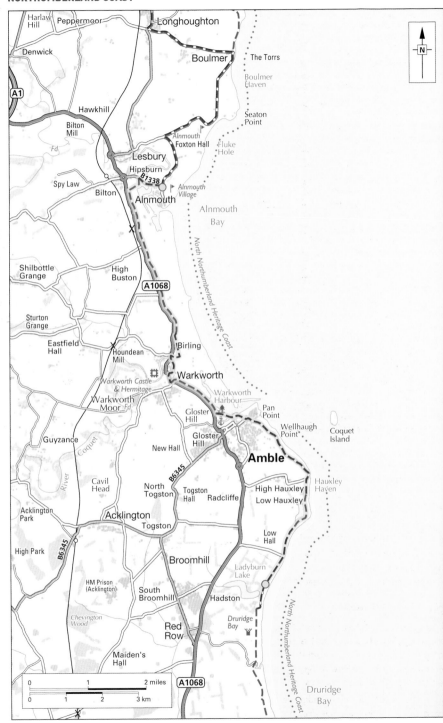

Warkworth Castle

routes, visit www.sustrans.org.uk
- Maps for this area are available to buy from www.sustransshop.co.uk
- **Amble Tourist Information:** 01665 712313; www.visitnorthumberland.com
- **Alnwick Tourist Information:** 01665 511333; www.visitnorthumberland.com
- **Northumberland Coast AONB:** www.northumberlandcoastaonb.org

ROUTE DESCRIPTION
Leave Alnmouth heading west on the B1338 Hipsburn Road. After the steel, arched bridge crossing the River Aln, turn left through a gated entrance onto a surfaced cyclepath. Continue to follow this for about a mile (1.6km) as it stays just inside a field boundary hedge next to the road, then turn left back towards the coastline,

following a coastal path to Warkworth. Passing the castle on your right, look for signs to Amble. Drop down the bank beside the A1068 and join a roadside pavement path alongside the River Coquet and weir. The signs will then lead you around through the marina, into the quieter streets of Amble and on past the harbour. Follow a traffic-calmed minor road to Low Hauxley and thereafter onto the stony coastal path to Druridge Bay.

NEARBY CYCLE ROUTES
This route forms part of the Coast & Castles Cycle Route between Newcastle-upon-Tyne and Edinburgh, part of National Route 1.

A guide to five cycle rides in the coastal AONB is available from the Northumberland Coast AONB (see above).

HOLY ISLAND – BERWICK-UPON-TWEED TO LINDISFARNE

The entire Coast & Castles Cycle Route runs between Newcastle-upon-Tyne and Aberdeen via Edinburgh. From Berwick-upon-Tweed, at the mouth of one of Britain's great salmon rivers, you can cycle the section that links it with Holy Island – often described as the 'jewel of the Northumberland coast'.

Throughout the Scottish Wars of Independence, strategically placed Berwick-upon-Tweed changed hands many times between Robert the Bruce, William Wallace and Edward I, somehow never finding itself on the right side. Despite Berwick being in the English county of Northumberland, Berwickshire itself is in Scotland, and the town's rugby and football teams both play in Scottish leagues.

It wasn't until the construction of the Ramparts – hugely expensive, state-of-the-art fortifications – by Elizabeth I that the town enjoyed some security and stability, but even now it is rumoured still to be at war with Russia by accidentally being excluded from an all-important treaty after the Crimean War.

Tear yourself away from checking out the town's history for a great view of the mouth of the Tweed, and head down the beautiful north Northumberland coastline to Holy Island, at the heart of the Lindisfarne National Nature Reserve.

Holy Island can be reached only via a 3-mile (5km) causeway. This is closed from two hours before high tide until three hours after, so check the tide tables in local newspapers or on the Northumberland County Council website before setting off. Tide times are also shown at the causeway.

Berwick-upon-Tweed harbour

ROUTE INFORMATION

National Route: 1
Start: Berwick-upon-Tweed train station.
Finish: Lindisfarne Priory.
Distance: 15 miles (24km).
Grade: Medium.
Surface: Tarmac on-road, and a mixture of stony track, grassy path and sealed-grit cycle track off-road. The stony track section south of Spittal is rough in places and may well be muddy in wet conditions.
Hills: None.

YOUNG & INEXPERIENCED CYCLISTS

Care is needed getting through Berwick town centre, in Tweedmouth and crossing the mainline railway at Cheswick. The coastline between Spittal and Holy Island is exposed to the elements, so overall this ride is better suited to older children, and best done in dry conditions and settled weather.

REFRESHMENTS

- Lots of choice in Berwick-upon-Tweed, Tweedmouth and Spittal.
- Pot-A-Doodle-Do cafe bistro, Scremerston.
- Coffee shop and restaurant at the Barn at Beal.
- Lots of choice on Holy Island.

THINGS TO SEE & DO

- **Berwick-upon-Tweed Castle:** remains of a medieval castle crucial to Anglo-Scottish warfare, demolished in 1843 by the North British Railway to make way for the present station; www.english-heritage.org.uk
- **Berwick-upon-Tweed Ramparts:** impressive bastioned defences; the circuit around the whole town can be walked; www.english-heritage.org.uk
- **The Barn at Beal, Beal Farm:** free visitor centre with spectacular views of Holy Island; outdoor trails; 01289 540044; www.barnatbeal.com
- **Lindisfarne Priory, Holy Island:** atmospheric ruins; original burial ground of St Cuthbert and still a place of pilgrimage; visitor centre; 01289 389200; www.english-heritage.org.uk
- **Lindisfarne Castle, Holy Island:** romantic 16th-century castle converted into an

Lindisfarne Castle, Holy Island

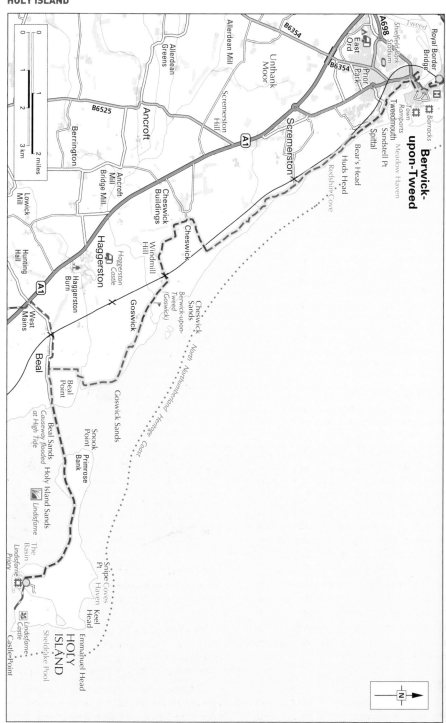

Edwardian home by Lutyens; spectacular views; 01289 389244; www.nationaltrust.org.uk

TRAIN STATIONS
Berwick-upon-Tweed.

BIKE HIRE
- Wilson Cycles, Berwick-upon-Tweed: 01289 331476

FURTHER INFORMATION
- To view or print National Cycle Network routes, visit www.sustrans.org.uk
- Maps for this area are available to buy from www.sustransshop.co.uk
- Berwick-upon-Tweed Tourist Information: 01289 301780; www.visitnorthumberland.com
  Northumberland Coast AONB: www.northumberlandcoastaonb.org

ROUTE DESCRIPTION
Turn right on leaving Berwick-upon-Tweed station and follow the blue signs for National Route 1 through the town to the quayside. Go over the 'old bridge' across the Tweed to Tweedmouth (the return route uses the 'new bridge'). Continue following the signs south along Dock Road through Spittal, where you pick up the coastal track leading along the cliffs to Cheswick. Having crossed the East Coast mainline railway as you enter Cheswick, look for a signed path leading you back towards the coast via a level crossing. This will lead you past the Goswick golf course and clubhouse and out towards Beachcomber House. Here you're on a grassy, then stony path across the headland to some sluice gates and a sealed-grit path, which connects to the causeway road to Holy Island.

Lindisfarne Priory

NEARBY CYCLE ROUTES
From Berwick-upon-Tweed, you can follow the 90-mile (143km) Tweed Cycle Route to Biggar (www.visitscottishborders.com), or you can head up the coast to Eyemouth and beyond on National Route 76, part of the Coast & Castles Cycle Route.

From Holy Island, the Coast & Castles Route takes in Bamburgh, Seahouses and Alnmouth (see page 118) on its way to Newcastle.

Berwick-upon-Tweed is the northern end of the Pennine Cycleway (National Route 68) and provides a link to Wooler market town on the edge of the Northumberland National Park.

NEXT STEPS...

We hope you have enjoyed the cycle rides in this book.

Sustrans developed the National Cycle Network to act as a catalyst for bringing cycling (and walking) back into our everyday lives. Between the 1950s and the mid-1970s cycling in the UK fell by 80%. Cycling now accounts for only about 2% of all journeys made in the UK, a fraction of what we used to achieve.

When you consider that nearly 6 in 10 car journeys are under 5 miles, it makes you wonder what the potential for increasing levels of cycling is. Evidence shows that, for local journeys under 5 miles, most of us could make 9 out of 10 journeys on foot, bike or public transport if there was more investment in making it possible to leave the car behind.

And why not? We can all be more savvy when it comes to travel. One small step becomes one giant leap if we all start walking away from less healthy lifestyles and pedalling our way towards happier children and a low carbon world.

And that's where Sustrans comes in. Sustainable travel means carbon-reducing, energy-efficient, calorie-burning, money-saving travel. Here are a few things that we think make sense. If you agree, join us.

- **Snail's pace** – 20mph or less on our streets where we live, go to school, shop and work – make it the norm, not just when there's snow or ice on the roads.

- **Closer encounters** – planning that focuses on good non-motorised access, so that we can reach more post offices, schools, shops, doctors and dentists without the car.

- **People spaces** – streets where kids can play hopscotch or football and be free-range, and where neighbours can meet and chat, and safe, local walking and cycling routes, to school and beyond.

- **Road revolution** – build miles and miles of bike paths that don't evaporate when they meet a road.

- **Find our feet** – campaign for pedestrian-friendly city centres, or wide boulevards with regular pedestrian crossings and slow-moving traffic.

- **Better buses** – used by millions, under-invested by billions and, if affordable, reliable and pleasant to use, could make local car journeys redundant.

- **More car clubs** – a car club on every street corner and several for every new-build estate.

- **Rewards for car-sharing** – get four in a car and take more than half the cars off the road.

- **Trains** – more of them, and cheaper.

- **Become a staycationer** – and holiday at home. Mountains, beaches, culture, great beer, good food and a National Cycle Network that connects them all.

If we work towards these goals we have a chance of delivering our fair share of the 80% reduction in CO_2 by mid-century that we're now committed to by law, and some of the 100% reduction that many climate experts now consider essential.

To find out more and join the movement, visit www.sustrans.org.uk

Free. Clean. Green.

Photo: Rita Platts/ Sustrans

Few people would say that they don't care about the environment, don't want to get fit or don't care about the damage pollution is doing to local communities – but what's the answer? The humble bike: a great way to get from A to B, cut carbon emissions and get fit at the same time. The bike is the greenest machine on the road, and Sustrans is doing everything it can to help people cycle more. Sustrans developed the National Cycle Network to help bring cycling (and walking) back into everyday life.

Cycling only accounts for 2% of all the journeys made in the UK today. 90% of all journeys under five miles could be made by foot, public transport or bike. And we are trying to do everything possible to make this happen. Help us provide everyone with a greener way to travel.

If you care about the environment and love cycling, you should support Sustrans. Get online at sustrans.org.uk, join the movement and find out how Sustrans can improve your cycling experience.

sustrans

JOIN THE MOVEMENT

ACKNOWLEDGEMENTS

Rupert Douglas would like to thank: Bryn Dowson, James Adamson, Neil Mitchell, David Hall, Peter Foster, Nikki Wingfield, Les Ford and David Gray for their help with the writing of this guide.

The Automobile Association would like to thank the following photographers, companies and picture libraries for their assistance in the preparation of this book.

Abbreviations for the picture credits are as follows – (t) top; (b) bottom; (l) left; (r) right; (c) centre; (dps) double page spread; (AA) AA World Travel Library

Front cover: Royal Border Railway Bridge; AA/J Hunt. Back cover: Wayne Hemingway; Sustrans.

3l Jon Bewley/Sustrans; 3r AA/Mike Kipling; 4 J Bewley/Sustrans; 5t AA/Caroline Jones; 5b Sustrans/ Cass Gilbert; 6/7 AA/Caroline Jones; 7tr AA/A Mockford & N Bonetti; 7ctr AA/Roger Coulam; 7cr AA/ Mike Kipling; 11tl Jon Bewley/Sustrans; 11tr Jon Bewley/Sustrans; 11c Jon Bewley/Sustrans; 11bc Andy Huntley/Sustrans; 11br Pru Comben/Sustrans; 13t Jon Bewley/Sustrans; 13c Nicola Jones/Sustrans; 13b Jon Bewley/Sustrans; 15t AA/Andy Midgley; 15c AA/Terry Marsh; 17 AA/Terry Marsh; 18 Alan Novelli/ Alamy; 19 Ed Rhodes/Alamy; 21tl Jack Sullivan/Alamy; 21tr Steve Allen Travel Photography/Alamy; 21b Alan Novelli/Alamy; 22/23 Mike Hewitt/Getty Images; 25 Ron Jones Associates/Merseyside Photo Library; 27 AA/Caroline Jones; 29l AA/Caroline Jones; 29r AA/ Caroline Jones; 30 Chris Bull/Alamy; 31 Adam James/ Alamy; 33 David Kennedy/Alamy; 35 Gareth Horne; 37t Gareth Horne; 37c Bryn Graves - www. brynphotography.co.uk; 38/39 Steven Gillis hd9 imaging/Alamy; 41t Steven Gillis hd9 imaging/Alamy; 41c David Hall/Sustrans; 42/43b John Morrison/Alamy; 43t Lancashire Images/Alamy; 45t AA/S&O Mathews; 45c Jon Bewley/Sustrans; 46 Ian Townsley/Alamy; 47t Jon Bewley/Sustrans; 47b Susan & Allan Parker/ Alamy; 48 Martin Pick/Alamy; 50t Robin Weaver/ Alamy; 50c Mike Kipling Photography/Alamy; 51 Leo Rosser/Alamy; 53l Jez Toogood/Sustrans; 53tr Jez Toogood/Sustrans; 53cr Paul Kirkwood/Sustrans; 54 AA/Linda Whitwam; 55t Paul Kirkwood/Sustrans; 55c Ryan McGinnis/Alamy; 57 Paul Kirkwood/Sustrans; 59 AA/D Clapp; 61t AA/John Morrison; 62/63b AA/Graham Rowatt; 63t Susan & Allan Parker/Alamy; 64 ICP/ Alamy; 67 Ashley Cooper/Alamy; 69 ICP-UK/Alamy; 70/71b AA/Caroline Jones; 71tr John Grimshaw/ Sustrans; 73 AA/Caroline Jones; 74 Jon Bewley/ Sustrans; 75l John Grimshaw/Sustrans; 75r Jon Bewley/Sustrans; 77 Kathy Bashford/Sustrans; 79t Stan Pritchard/Alamy; 79c John Grimshaw/Sustrans; 81 AA/A Mockford & N Bonetti; 82/83 incamerastock/ Alamy; 86/87 Graeme Peacock/Alamy; 87tr David Martin/Sustrans; 89 Andy Hay (rspb-images.com); 91t AA/Mike Kipling; 91c John Grimshaw/Sustrans; 93t AA/Mike Kipling; 93c AA/Mike Kipling; 94 Mike Kipling Photography/Alamy; 95 Mike Kipling Photography/ Alamy; 97 Mike Kipling Photography/Alamy; 98 Paul Kirkwood/Sustrans; 99 Mike Kipling Photography/ Alamy; 100l Peter Jordan_NE/Alamy; 100/101 Alan Curtis/Alamy; 102 Roger Coulam/Alamy; 103t travelib prime/Alamy; 103c Stuart Forster/Alamy; 105 AA/Jeff Beazley; 106/107 NTPL/Robert Morris; 107 Matt Davies/Sustrans; 108 Jason Friend Photography Ltd/ Alamy; 110 AA/Roger Coulam; 111t AA/Tim Woodcock; 111b AA/Roger Coulam; 113 AA; 114/115b David Taylor Photography/Alamy; 115tr David Taylor Photography/ Alamy; 117t AA/Roger Coulam; 117c Brian Swinburne/ Alamy; 118/119 AA/Roger Coulam; 121 AA/Roger Coulam; 122 Graeme Peacock/Alamy; 123 AA/ Cameron Lees; 125 AA/Jeff Beazley.

Every effort has been made to trace the copyright holders, and we apologise in advance for any unintentional omissions or errors. We would be pleased to apply any corrections in the following edition of this publication.